Transculturation and Resistance in Lusophone African Narrative

Transculturation and Resistance in Lusophone African Narrative

Phyllis Peres

University Press of Florida
Gainesville/Tallahassee/Tampa/Boca Raton
Pensacola/Orlando/Miami/Jacksonville

02 01 00 99 98 97   6 5 4 3 2 1

Library of Congress Cataloging-in-Publication Data

Peres, Phyllis, 1953–
Transculturation and resistance in lusophone African narrative /
Phyllis Peres.
p. cm.
Includes bibliographical references and index.
ISBN 0-8130-1492-1 (cloth: alk. paper)
1. African fiction (Portuguese)—History and criticism
I. Title.
PQ9904.P47 1997   96-20868
869.3—dc20

The University Press of Florida is the scholarly publishing agency for the State University System of
Florida, comprised of Florida A & M University, Florida Atlantic University, Florida International
University, Florida State University, University of Central Florida, University of Florida, University
of North Florida, University of South Florida, and University of West Florida.

University Press of Florida
15 Northwest 15th Street
Gainesville, FL 32611

Contents

Preface

One of the first critical commentaries on Lusophone African literatures contends that "literature in the Portuguese language was the earliest written in Black Africa, but it has remained the last to be discovered."[1] This claim by Gerald Moser, a pioneering scholar of Lusophone African literatures, is still valid for several reasons. Undoubtedly, the most compelling factor is the still relatively obscure position of Portuguese language and literary-cultural studies in the United States. This obscurity is compounded by the lack of English-language translations of Lusophone African literary texts. With the exception of several noteworthy translations, and even fewer substantial critical works in English, the literatures of Angola, Mozambique, Cape Verde, Guinea-Bissau, and São Tomé e Príncipe are "undiscovered" in the United States.

This book intends to help bridge that critical gap in contemporary African literature studies in this country. Specifically, my work focuses on the fiction of several contemporary Angolan writers whose narratives are fundamental to an understanding of that nation's social and cultural history. The time frame of my study is essential. It starts with the period in which Angolan nationalist movements began a protracted liberation struggle against the Portuguese colonial regime. Independence was achieved in 1975, but Angola has been torn apart by civil war in the two decades since then.

Undoubtedly the works of many Angolan writers in the immediate pre-independence era collaborate in the acute confrontations—cultural and otherwise—that marked the end of colonialism in Angola. Narratives by contemporary Angolan fiction writers engage and are engaged in these confrontations, although not from the perspective of merely denying colonial identity. Writers such as Luandino Vieira, Pepetela, Uanhenga Xitu, Manuel Rui, and others who emerged from the nationalist struggle in Angola produced both poetry and fiction that did indeed negate colonial identity, but more relevant to this study, they also participated in the textualization of an Angolan nation, or perhaps more aptly phrased, Angolan nationness.

In this book I explain how Angolan fiction narrates the emerging nation from the early 1960s to the mid-1990s. Essential to this project is the questioning provoked by various critical perspectives on colonial and postcolonial textualizations of nation and nationness, as well as on the constructs of nationalism. I focus on the problematics of mapping the borders of national identities and communities. How do contemporary Angolan narratives imagine the emerging nation? How do identities of race, class, gender, and ethnicity chart the boundaries of collective selfhood?

Also central to my study of imagining Angola is how nationness is textualized in narratives of resistance. Barbara Harlow's work on resistance literature suggests that the narrative discourse of resistance redefines the cultural images of a given historical moment, not only to expose symbolic structures of colonial domination but also to open up possible futures.[2] Resistance narratives are necessarily violent, certainly in Fanon's sense of the counterviolence of liberation,[3] but also as strategies in reclaiming contested discursive terrain. These narratives are meaningful primarily as they textualize resistance as a collective practice of discovering the boundaries of national subjectivities. It is precisely at this junction of resistance and imagination that I seek to explore Angolan writing as border narrative, not in the strict delineating sense of mapping a borderline but rather as an indeterminate borderland practice.

In the first chapter I raise these and other questions concerning the critical boundaries of narrating nation in the context of resistance literature and revolutionary production. Four subsequent chapters each are devoted to specific narratives by Luandino Vieira, Uanhenga Xitu, Pepetela, and Manuel Rui that engage in the varied imaginings of Angolan selfhood. Luandino Vieira's narrative texts date from 1957 to 1972, most written while the author was interned at the Portuguese camp for political prisoners at Tarrafal, Cape Verde. His prison writing is the violent narrative defiance of transculturation, the counternarrative to colonial texts of acculturation and creolization. In many ways, his narratives have come to influence a whole generation of Angolan fiction writers, particularly in regard to the development of new textual forms that incorporate Kimbundu orature.

At first glance, Uanhenga Xitu's writing proposes a cultural nationalist stance as his texts recover disappearing traditional practices. The more important glance, however, is Xitu's own as it deflects European visions of otherness from within the very ambiguities of colonial discourse. His narratives are no less ambivalent as they construct their differences through the double vision of mimicry.

Pepetela, whose most recent narrative appeared in 1995, has long been concerned with the indeterminate spaces of Angolan selfhood and the synthesis of numerous cultures at the national level. His works, dating from the late 1960s to the mid-1990s, always are critical configurations of nation that voice the tensions of revolutionary productivity. Several of his pre-independence narratives are utopic projections into a future postcolonial Angola, as the imaginings of nation as a privileged hybrid terrain. Pepetela's most recent post-independence works are still projections into the near future, but they make problematic the viability of nation, given the sharp divisions that have marked postcolonial Angola.

Manuel Rui's book-length narratives are mostly postcolonial and are positioned on the borders of national independence and nationhood. His texts engage the euphoric moments of nationness as well as the ironic visions of national formation as the revolution is betrayed. His narratives perhaps more than anyone else's manipulate the emerging codes of Angolan nationness as both euphoria and irony.

Obviously, I do not intend to put forth a general prescription for how nation is constructed in contemporary Angolan narrative. What underlies the texts of all of these writers, however, is their imaginings of nation as open-ended narratives. These are narratives without closure that do not so much end as point to possible futures. In this sense, their final punctuation is more of a question mark than a period, so that narrative threads are oftentimes left dangling, to be picked up again and reimagined. Like the oral tales that have informed much of contemporary Angolan fiction, these narratives are for re-telling; they are multivoiced and multilayered, as are their textualizations of nation. In the narrations of a syncretized and hybrid Angola, nation is imagined as community but not as a horizontal leveling of race, gender, class, and ethnicity. The imaginings themselves, open-ended as they remain, are always problematic and often ambivalent, but nonetheless as narratives of resistance they resonate possibilities of utopic futures.

In the last two chapters, I also study how post-independence Angolan narratives have questioned the supposedly liberating condition of postcolonialism as a historical moment of closure. Utopian visions of imagined nation here are counterposed by dystopian realities in the nation-space. While still narrating nationness, postcolonial Angolan texts often are self-critical interventions into the records of promises and failures as well as the devastation of ethnic and geopolitical factionalisms. As such, they ultimately question nation itself and invoke a type of postnationalism as they reimagine the borderlands of Angolan selfhood and its possible futures.

There are many acknowledgments to be made. Institutional funding from the Calouste Gulbenkian and Fulbright-Hays Foundations allowed me to complete early archival research in Lisbon. A University of Maryland General Research Board Grant provided me with valuable time for rewriting. I could not have written this book without the input of the four writers themselves. Luandino Vieira, Uanhenga Xitu, Pepetela, and Manuel Rui all took time out of their busy schedules in Angola and elsewhere to meet with me and discuss their works. I am especially grateful to Luandino Vieira, who in his capacity as head of the Angolan Writers Union facilitated interviews and meetings. I also thank him for taking me on Mais-Velho's narrative path through Luanda. Other Angolan writers and critics such as Arnaldo Santos, E. Bonavena, and Luís Kandjimbo also were generous with their time and help.

In Portugal, I am greatly indebted to Joaquim Soares da Costa of Edições 70 for both bibliographic material and invaluable assistance in traveling to Luanda. The late Portuguese writer and critic Manuel Ferreira, himself a pioneering scholar of Lusophone Africa, most graciously provided research space and encouragement.

Over the years and in various places, many colleagues and friends have provided intellectual support and camaraderie. I thank them all. In particular, Russell Hamilton has encouraged this book from its very beginning stages. He has been a continued source of inspiration, advice, and support for those of us writing on Lusophone Africa and to me as a mentor and friend. I am also grateful to Jane Malinoff Kamide with whom I first read African-Brazilian and Angolan literature and whose friendship is unmatched.

Finally, I thank my family for patience and understanding. My sister, Leonor, encouraged my interest in Spanish and Portuguese literatures at an early age. My daughter, Kamilia, always recomposed my narrowing universe. My partner, David, gave much support and advice. He also read everything I wrote—at least twice! I am grateful to them all.

Chapter 1

The History and Context
of Contemporary Angolan Narratives

Transculturation and Resistance

> Thus, it may seem that if imperialist domination has the vital need
> to practice cultural oppression, national liberation is necessarily an
> act of culture.
> Amílcar Cabral, *National Liberation and Culture*

Portuguese Domination and Acculturation

All borderland writing has a history and a context. In the case of Angola that
history is one of Portuguese domination and Angolan resistance that began in
1483 when Diogo Cão's expedition arrived at the Zaire estuary in the Kongo
Kingdom. That initial encounter led to the establishment of a Christian stronghold often referred to as "the Kongo experiment."[1] The contact may have
begun auspiciously, at least in terms of imperial expansion, but it soon took
on another light as the Portuguese turned to more lucrative enterprises in
India. Under the Christian kingdom of the Manikongo Afonso I, the Kongo
became a commercial dependency of São Tomé, at that time a center for
sugar production and the slave trade. The letters written by Afonso to the
king of Portugal that asked for the means to protect the Kongo against the
slavers of São Tomé are among the first African writings in Portuguese.[2] Those
letters were either intercepted in São Tomé or they received inadequate re-
sponses.

The failure of the Kongo experiment, the initial Portuguese venture into
what is now Angola, serves in many ways as a paradigm for five hundred years
of Portuguese domination in the region. Arriving in Angola on the eve of the
Reformation and Counter-Reformation, the Portuguese brought the promises of a Catholicism that would grant salvation, a mercantilism that would

generate wealth, and a superior culture that would supersede and enlighten. The reality, of course, was that the promise of mercantilism opened the door to São Tomense slave traders and the beginnings of the Atlantic slave trade that would devastate the Angola-Kongo region for the next three hundred and fifty years. Instead of salvation, the Catholic Church provided an ideological patina to justify the exploitation and colonization of the region. And the promises of a superior culture masked the harsh realities of deculturation that would continue until national independence in 1975.

For the Portuguese, the Kongo experiment was a first step in what would later be defined as a "Christian civilizing mission" that presupposed the inferiority of autochthonous African cultures. Colonial policies of assimilation and acculturation that were implemented to accomplish this mission involved an assertion of Portuguese cultural superiority and a deculturation of colonized peoples. Although assimilation programs were largely unsuccessful throughout the extended Portuguese presence in Angola, the effects of this attempted acculturation continued to figure prominently in Angolan nationalism.

Portuguese strategies for acculturation varied from colony to colony and over time. In terms of twentieth-century colonial policies in Africa, economist Eduardo de Sousa Ferreira makes a basic distinction between settler colonies—Angola and Mozambique—and colonies exploited primarily for goods— Cape Verde, Guinea-Bissau, and São Tomé e Príncipe. Ferreira does not conceive of Angola and Mozambique merely as settler colonies, but rather he uses this distinction to explain the effects of Portuguese colonialism upon the cultures of the colonized societies. For the most part, in the *colónias de exploração* (colonies of exploitation), the Portuguese presence was limited to colonial officials and merchants, so that the interference with autochthonous cultural practices was less extensive.[3]

In the specific case of Angola, the settler aspect of Portuguese colonization was introduced as a large-scale measure relatively late and, despite efforts by the Portuguese government to promote a rural colonial population, was largely limited to urban areas.[4] During the early decades of the twentieth century, Portugal was reluctant to invest capital in the African colonies, and by 1930 both Angola and Mozambique were virtually bankrupt. The formation of the Portuguese New State, however, redefined colonial policy through a regeneration of imperial consciousness that was implemented by the 1930 Colonial Act as well as by subsequent decrees. In the decades that followed, both Angola and Mozambique became "white men's colonies."[5]

When the Colonial Act became law there were some 30,000 Portuguese settlers in Angola. By the outbreak of armed insurrection in 1961, that population had soared to more than 170,000, with the largest increase during the 1950s. This post–World War II influx of settlers from the metropolis occurred during the same period in which African nationalist movements were undertaking liberation struggles and other European powers were coming to terms, in one way or another, with the independence of their African colonies.

The increase in number of Portuguese settlers in Angola had several immediate effects. Most of these Portuguese were unskilled workers who remained in segregated areas in the urban centers and, as a result, drastically altered the established settlement patterns of those areas. In addition, the vast increase of unskilled labor in the cities caused a displacement of African workers, which provoked racial tensions and stimulated ideological justification of socioeconomic privileges on the basis of color.

Previously, the limited presence of Portuguese settlers in Angola had permitted the development of a type of creolized society in urban areas, particularly in Luanda.[6] Russell Hamilton notes that this incipient creolized society that flourished from the mid-nineteenth century to the beginning of the twentieth century formed the basis for what would become a petit bourgeoisie composed of whites, mestizos, and "assimilated" blacks.[7] Members of this bourgeoisie were active as writers and journalists during that period. Further, the first texts of revindication, protest, and protonationalism emerged during this era and reflect the sociopolitical and cultural ambivalences of this creolized bourgeoisie. The colonial policies of the Portuguese New State and the boom in the white settler population greatly reduced patterns of creolization and the accessibility of class ascendancy to all but a limited number of Angolan blacks and mestizos.

This aspect of Portuguese colonial domination in Angola is crucial, since it was from this very basis—the creation of a harmonious, racially mixed, pan-Lusitanian society—that Portugal sought to justify its presence in Africa in the face of growing unrest in the colonies and increased worldwide criticism. In his study on Portuguese domination, Américo Boavida identifies this final stage of Portugal's colonial ideology as "the divine mission of a chosen people" in its fight against communist expansion.[8] This stage was further mystified by the elaboration of an ideology of "multiracialism," originally developed by Gilberto Freyre to explain the unique character of Brazil's multiracial society.

Gilberto Freyre introduced the "science of tropical space-time" based on the distinction between the colonialist expansion propagated by imperial economic European nations (European ethnocentric) and Hispanic colonization, in particular, that of Portugal, which was Luso-Christocentric. In 1957 Freyre described the Lusotropical civilizations in America, Africa, and Asia as subareas that "form a single system of living and culture" characterized by assimilation of tropical values into European culture maintained by the "Portuguese." Here Freyre means either "social" or "cultural" Portuguese "who can be either yellow, dark, red, black, or white" because the ethnic condition is superseded by the common culture. Indeed, for Freyre, this is precisely what characterizes Lusoptropical civilizations.[9] Of course Freyre, by that time, was writing as an apologist for Portuguese colonization and a defender of what he saw as Lusotropical societies in formation.

In Portugal, Lusotropicalism as a theory was officially propagated late in the history of Portuguese colonialism. Indeed the whole concept of multiracialism, originally developed in the 1930s, was soundly rejected at that time by the Portuguese. However late Portuguese ideologues adopted the theory of multiracialism in support of an autonomous pan-Lusitanian nation, that theory shares essential affinities with earlier colonial expansionist ideologies that defended the Portuguese Christian civilizing mission as one that was not economically motivated. In an often overlooked essay on Portuguese domination, Perry Anderson describes this latter ideology as an indicator of the uniqueness of Portuguese colonial imperialism. In effect, according to Anderson, real differences within colonial history that were established by cultural and economic patterns of early Portuguese imperialism have been distorted by a colonial ideology that misinterprets and mystifies those very differences. For instance, the negation of an economically motivated colonialism refracts Portuguese underdevelopment and lack of capital. In the same manner, the espousal of a multiracial pan-Lusitanian society based on racial tolerances distorts the sociohistorical contexts for early patterns of miscegenation.[10]

In terms of the cultural aspects of Portuguese colonial domination and ideology, from the time that the first Portuguese expedition arrived in the Angola-Kongo region at the end of the fifteenth century, Portugal's declared mission was to spread a more advanced civilization and culture. Defenders of Portuguese imperialism regarded this early contact as one that established essential colonial patterns of education, Christianization, and economic development. Ironically, of course, the colonial apologists were correct. From the beginning of the Portuguese presence in Angola, the so-called civilizing mission, at first accepted in good faith by the Manikongo, was offset by the establishment of the slave trade in which missionaries participated. It was the last time that the Portuguese attempted a peaceful alliance based on cultural assimilation. From the seventeenth century on, Portuguese policy in Angola was defined, as Duffy describes it, by "exploitation of the African mass coupled with a paternalistic acceptance of the African or mulatto minority who came to share Portuguese cultural values."[11]

The policy of cultural assimilation was always a cornerstone of Portuguese colonial ideology. In the implementation of that ideology, the term *assimilado* (assimilated) became a legal category to classify those "indigenous" people who had assimilated Portuguese cultural values. The Native Assistance Code of 1921 provides one of the first legal definitions of assimilado as being able to speak Portuguese, having forsaken all tribal customs, and being gainfully employed.[12] In 1930, the Regime do Indigenato (Regime for Indigenous Peoples) established with the Colonial Act divided the population into two categories, *indígenas* and *não-indígenas* (indigenous and nonindigenous), and while the category of assimilado was not legally codified, it existed as part of the nonindigenous sector.

Theoretically, the Regime do Indigenato was meant to serve as the juridical means of implementing a selective process of cultural assimilation for those who would seek their identity with Portugal. In reality, the 1930 legislation represented a turning point in Portuguese imperialism in terms of its economic expansion and labor practices, as well as the propagation of Portuguese culture. Douglas Wheeler, who has written extensively on the history of assimilation policies in Angola and the role of assimilados in the development of Angolan nationalism, explains that the *indigenato* system that was enforced until 1961 signaled the end of the nineteenth-century liberal approach, which assumed that Africans would be naturally adapted into the Portuguese sector. Wheeler in fact argues that this was the modern expression of Portugal's civilizing mission.[13]

In this sense, the rather late incorporation of Freyre's theory of Lusotropicalism into colonial ideology serves as a means of substantiating an assimilation policy that was upheld as culturally, rather than racially or ethnically, selective. Eduardo de Sousa Ferreira convincingly argues that the very legal mechanism by which the Portuguese sought to disguise racial categories as cultural ones carried its own negation. The category of assimilado was applied strictly in racial terms, since all Portuguese in Angola were automatically considered part of the *civilizado* (civilized) sector. As Ferreira points out, the vast majority of the Portuguese population would not have been able to meet a criterion of cultural assimilation because they were illiterate.[14]

However, the assertion that the process of assimilation was based on racial rather than cultural categories does not deny the real impact of colonial cultural domination. In 1950, only 30,000 Africans (0.7 percent) were officially registered as não-indígenas, compared to 100 percent of the white population and 88.8 percent of the mestizos. While these statistics reveal that the vast majority of Africans remained classified as *não-civilizados* (noncivilized), the complexities of cultural assimilation merit closer examination. Gerald Bender points out that while it was theoretically possible for any African or mestizo to become legally classified as nonindigenous, the main reason for the small number of assimilados was that few Africans had access to institutions that could impart Portuguese civilization. Indeed, as Bender concludes, "Angola had scarcely any institutions which could contribute to the civilization of either Africans, mestiços or Europeans."[15]

Critics of cultural assimilation policies in Angola have emphasized that the 1961 colonial reform that abolished the juridical mechanisms distinguishing between indígenas and não-indígenas in reality had little effect on the establishment or accessibility of such institutions. This holds especially true in the area of education, supposedly the primary mechanism for the implementation of cultural assimilation. Discrimination against Africans in education continued after 1961, particularly by means of social and financial obstacles. In addition, the Portuguese still failed to support the establishment of primary and secondary schools.[16]

Ironically, the Portuguese strongly believed that their colonization was nonracist and nonexploitative in practice, and as Gerald Bender states, "It followed that anything that broke down traditional African institutions, beliefs, and practices—including forced labor—was positive since it took Africans farther away from their own cultures and closer to the Portuguese way of life."[17] The failure to establish institutions that would provide access to Portuguese civilizations and culture, in addition to the fact that separate education programs for Africans and whites continued even after the 1961 reform, demonstrates sociocultural underdevelopment. It also has been argued that this underdevelopment was intentional, especially in the area of education. The history of Portuguese colonialism in Africa, in fact, has been often described in terms of an underdevelopment not only related to Portugal's own history of social and economic dependency, but also to the repression in Portugal itself during the regime of the New State.

The various factors of Portuguese colonial history thus far introduced— the failure, by and large, of the civilizing mission; the late arrival of a large, unskilled, white settler population; the implementation of the policies of cultural assimilation; and the inaccessibility to institutions that would impart Portuguese culture—indicate that the majority of the African population in Angola remained apart from Portuguese cultural values. This is not to deny, however, the profound effects of Portuguese colonial practices on African cultures. As Bender emphasizes, "Any policy or activity which destroyed traditional African institutions, settlement patterns or beliefs was perceived by most Portuguese as inherently good, even magnanimous!"[18] An even more scathing indictment of the colonial order appears in Basil Davidson's *In the Eye of the Storm: Angola's People*. Davidson contends that Portuguese colonialism caused a dismantlement of traditional social formations through forced-labor practices, the destruction of indigenous governments, and the imposition of commercialized cultures.[19]

What is essential here, regardless of the measurable outcome of the civilizing mission or its cultural assimilation policies, is that this mission was intrinsic to Portugal's own view of itself as a nation. Furthermore, within the final stages of Portuguese domination in Angola, acculturation of the "inferior Other" served as a strategy for recharting the borders of Portuguese nationness precisely at that moment in which Angolans were mapping their own boundaries of national selfhood.

Angolan Resistance and Transculturation

If acculturation was the strategy developed by Portugal to erase the boundary between a Portuguese empire and an imagined pan-Lusitanian nation, then the failure of that same strategy left the boundary intact, as indeed in practice it always was. This boundary, however, for contemporary Angolan nationalists was not between empire and metropolitan space but rather between colony and an imagined liberated nation.

These two very differently conceived boundaries had profound implications for the development of literary practices in post–World War II Angola. It is no coincidence that while the Portuguese New State was "discovering" Angola imaginatively if not literally,[20] the cultural-literary movement of the Generation of 1950 also sought to "discover Angola."[21] While the Portuguese sought to discover an Angola that mirrored in some fashion the culture of the geographical mainland, the Angolans wanted to discover a culture that might define the borders of potential nation-space.

This search to discover an Angolan national culture represents a distinct break from assimilationist strategies of past Angolan intellectual movements. During the free press era of the mid-nineteenth to early twentieth centuries, numerous journals and newspapers were established in Angola, including several that were edited by assimilated blacks and mestizos. Several of these publications did indeed criticize Portuguese colonial practices but were melioristic rather than resistant. Douglas Wheeler specifically refers to the mestizo journalist José Fontes Pereira, who published articles in O Futuro de Angola and O Arauto Africano, as the first assimilado to publish radical criticism of Portuguese colonial policies. Wheeler admits, however, that "the cultural patterns of the Angolan assimilado were almost exclusively and consciously Portuguese, and in effect, assimilados were often Black Portuguese."[22] While several publications during the free press period did serve as forums for criticism of Portuguese colonial rule, the majority of criticism, even that which can be termed protonationalist, was directed toward Portugal's failure to carry out effectively and justly its civilizing mission. The notion of Angola as nation, either politically or culturally, did not figure at all in these critiques.

Wheeler's assessment does demand further study, though, especially as it pertains to literary and nonliterary works by such writers as Cordeiro da Matta and Assis Júnior.[23] Although these works point to a conscious assimilation of Portuguese cultural values, they also are marked by aspects of the same cultural ambivalence that characterized that period's urban creolized society as a whole. Moreover, this is not to say that writers such as Assis Júnior were not equally conscious of their own ambiguous position but rather that these creolized patterns emerged in spite of assumed textual positions of cultural purism, separatism, or even protonationalism.

The position of the assimilado, always tenuous in colonial Angola, was effectively undermined in the 1920s, particularly during the second regime of High Commissioner Norton de Matos (1921–24). Assimilado organizations, such as the Liga Angolana and the Grêmio Africano, were banned, as were assimilado publications. Furthermore, with the establishment of the Portuguese New State, such organizations had to be approved and sponsored by the state. Wheeler argues that the demise of the Portuguese First Republic in 1926 ended an important phase of Angolan nationalism in which moderate assimilados were silenced and deported.[24]

Twenty-five years later, the Luanda-based journal *Mensagem* (1951–52) published some of the literary works of the new cultural-literary movement and was banned by the Portuguese government after only two issues.[25] This time, however, the colonial regime was unable to silence the voices that participated in this new phase of Angolan nationalism. The 1950s writers created new outlets for their creative works in journals such as *Cultura* (Luanda, 1957–61) and in publications edited by the Casa dos Estudantes do Império in Lisbon.[26]

More important, the times and the voices were different. One of these differences was the multiracial composition of the Generation of 1950. In *Literatura Africana, Literatura Necessária*, Russell Hamilton attributes this participation of white Angolan writers in the anticolonial movement to the peculiarities of Portuguese colonialism. As Hamilton explains, these white "rebels" in Angola were drawn mostly from the lower classes, and they joined with African and mestizo intellectuals in the attempt to revindicate the rights of the mass of Angola's African population.[27] There are several possible reasons why white Angolan writers of this period identified with African nationalism in ways that white writers in other African colonies did not. Many of these writers, as will be discussed in chapter 2, grew up in the *musseques* (African neighborhoods) before these gave way to the Europeanized neighborhoods of the incoming white settlers. In addition, they were politically socialists and identified themselves with the socialist liberation strategies of their African and mestizo counterparts. Finally, the very fascist rigidity of the Portuguese New State provided no meliorist possibility.

Another more important difference lies in the nature of the themes and issues with which the Generation of 1950 was concerned. These writers were engaged in a process that Amílcar Cabral describes as a "cultural reconversion." For Cabral, cultural contestation was the necessary first phase of any liberation struggle and involved the re-Africanization of elements of the colonized elite.[28] Here, re-Africanization requires the nationalist or revolutionary intellectual vanguard to identify with the cultural and social values of the African masses. As pertains to the 1950s cultural-literary movement in Angola, the identification with Angolan culture required these writers to identify not only the African masses but to define what Angolan culture was in the first instance.

The struggle on the part of these writers to discover Angolan mass culture is evident in the poetry of the time, which is replete with images of Mother Africa and the African earth as well as with poetic depictions of such colonial exploitation as contract labor and displacement. More important, these works incorporate the voices of allegedly authentic Angolan speakers as they are imagined to be. In some instances, there is a certain sense of self-consciousness of the sort that Gayatri Spivak discusses in "Can the Subaltern Speak?" concerning the dangers of essentialist strategies on the part of nationalist intellectuals who attempt to speak for subaltern masses.[29] Such intellectuals might engage in the creation of a monolithic subaltern mass whose voice duplicates that of elite nationalists when in fact subalterns may have their own particular strategies for resistance and liberation and may speak in many voices rather than a single voice. Agostinho Neto, for example, writes in "Mussunda Amigo" of the separation between the intellectual and the subaltern and stresses that there are different paths to liberation. In this poem, the poetic voice is so distanced from that of his friend that the latter cannot even read the verses that the poet is writing. The disparate elements come together in the poem, though, in the formation of a "we" that may travel along different paths but is one in the goal of liberation.

In another poem, Neto writes in the voice of a *quitandeira* (vendor) who sells not only oranges but herself. Her labor and her life are taken by the colonial ruling class, but ironically she gives her pain and her voice to the poets themselves so that she disappears completely in the process.

As part of cultural contestation, these poems not only participate in radical critiques of imposed patterns of acculturated identity, but also seek to discover the borders of a collective Angolan selfhood. Barbara Harlow describes resistance poetry as engaged in the struggle to preserve and ultimately redefine the cultural images that underwrite collective action.[30] The poetry of the Generation of 1950 is very much an integral part of contemporary Angolan resistance as it attacks the symbolic and imagined frontiers of Portuguese nationness expressed through strategies of acculturation. Moreover, this attack poses its own symbolic structures and borders, not through acculturated discourse but rather through strategies of transculturation.

Transculturation, as Mary Louise Pratt explains in her work on travel writing, was a concept developed in 1947 by Cuban anthropologist Fernando Ortiz in his groundbreaking study on Afro-Cuban culture and incorporated into literary studies by Angel Rama in the 1970s.[31] Generally speaking, transculturation describes the processes through which oppressed, colonized, or peripheral cultures transform imposed metropolitan or dominant cultural practices and elements. In a critical sense, transculturation is important as it counters the colonial or dominant practices presumed with acculturation as well as the uncomplicated synthesis often assumed with either creolization or *mestiçagem*.

Transculturation, I would argue, is particularly useful in this study as an intellectual framework for understanding the processes by which Angolan narratives both appropriate and transform dominant Portuguese discourse. In this sense, it opposes the framework explicit in acculturation that assumes a static tension between indigenous cultural discourse and the presumedly superior metropolitan mode. The model of acculturation assumes a false dichotomy in which practices must be either native or that of the colonizer. Transculturation assumes a fluidity, however tense and ambiguous, that functions in both directions. Although the focus of this study is not on how the colony determined or changed discourse in the metropolis itself, in fact discourse in Luanda influenced Lisbon just as modes of discourse in Lisbon played a necessary part in the development of a distinctly Angolan mode of imagining nation. This fluidity, of course, counters Portugal's colonial constructs of nation and related strategies of acculturation as a means of domination. The Portuguese term *cafrealizado* (from *kaffir*), used pejoratively to describe an "Africanized" settler, is illustrative of the way in which the colonizers understood acculturation as a strictly one-way process.

I would further propose that beginning with the Generation of 1950, strategies of transculturation not only speak to the negation of acculturated colonial identity but also to what the Angolan writer Mário Pinto de Andrade described as Angola's cultural dualism.[32] This cultural divergence is, of course, due to the colonial failure to inculcate Portuguese culture within the widespread rural sectors of Angola. Studies by Henrique Abranches as well as others indicate that while Portuguese culture and civilization were not made available to the vast majority of Africans, Portuguese colonial practices had a devastating impact on traditional cultures, and that resistance was widespread even in the rural sectors.[33] Although the analysis of patterns of cultural resistance in traditional practices is beyond the scope of this study, contemporary writers such as Agostinho Neto and others were concerned with the problem of cultural division, especially in regard to the construction of national identity.

Transculturation, then, would further complicate the context in which Angolan writers textualized nationness, particularly the tense transformations of both imposed and local cultures. Rather than participate in the idealized "return to the traditional sources" so profoundly criticized by both Fanon and Cabral, Angolan nationalists from the 1950s on engaged in strategies of transculturation to counter the divisionary tactics of colonial acculturation. If these nationalist writers sought to map the boundaries of Angolan selfhood, it was clear from even this beginning phase of contemporary nationalism that "selfhood" was not only to be set off against the assimilated identity of colonization but also would incorporate disparate cultures within the imagined nation itself.

Acts of Culture

On December 10, 1975, Agostinho Neto, the first president of Angola, spoke at the opening ceremony of the União dos Escritores Angolanos (Angolan Writers Union, or UEA) in an address that emphasized the cultural dimension of the national liberation struggle: "The struggle for national liberation must not separate itself from the struggle for the imposition and recognition of a culture particular to our people." [34]

This brief fragment of Neto's speech at the founding of the Angolan Writers Union just one month following independence is, in fact, very telling of several facets of Angolan nationalism. At the least, it indicates the vanguard position of militant writers within the liberation movement that ultimately proclaimed the nation. Angolan writers, including Agostinho Neto himself, figured dynamically within the ranks and leadership of the Movimento Popular de Libertação de Angola (Popular Movement for the Liberation of Angola, or MPLA) and would continue to do so after independence in the political party of the same name.

Neto's phrasing is solidly engaged in the public discourse of nationalism that proclaims the heterogenous many as the monolithic national one. This homogenization of "Angolanness" of "the people" posits national selfhood as uncomplicated precisely at the complex historical moment of Angolan nationhood. If Neto's strategy is to celebrate the unity of Angola's people, the disunity of the liberation struggle evidenced by the already ongoing civil war as well as the proclamation of nation itself loom menacingly and not in the shadows but in the forefront. As discursive strategy, political liberation is inextricably linked to cultural revindication as the imposition of a culture that is particular to the people.

Nationalist rhetoric aside, for the moment, Neto's linking of political and cultural liberation reveals one variation of Angolan resistance to colonial domination and, of course, is apropos to the occasion. Not only were militant writers active within the MPLA, but it also has been effectively argued that their texts were arms in the struggle itself.[35] The occasion may cause Neto to particularize about cultural resistance but does not detract from its primacy within the nationalist struggle. In this sense, Neto's speech echoes that of Amílcar Cabral cited at the opening of this chapter. For Cabral, the liberation struggle is itself "an act of culture," at least in terms of reclaiming cultural space.

Undoubtedly this reclamation, as Edward Said asserts in *Culture and Imperialism*, is at the center of decolonization as "the charting of cultural territory."[36] Said's imagery here is important, first as a countermapping to the seemingly rigid colonial boundaries of political and cultural terrain. The countermapping is only part of the reoccupation of restricted territory that was reserved for the European (in this case, the Portuguese) and prohibited for the "inferior Other." For Cabral as well as Said, who cites the late African nationalist leader and theorist extensively, the violent breakdown of colonial boundaries is the process through which the colonized subjects reintegrate their history as both communal and national.

Following Said's argument that colonial narratives were an unconcealed part of the European imperial process in the nineteenth and twentieth centuries, I would propose, in the case of Angola, that nationalist texts engaged in retaking cultural terrain as part of the process of decolonization. As such, these texts were not reflective of the nationalist movement in Angola but rather were works of resistance that battled for cultural territory as much as armed revolution sought to liberate the colonized geographical terrain. For Angolan resistance literature, narratives were the very sites in which history was reclaimed and reexamined.

Barbara Harlow's work on resistance literature demonstrates that across national boundaries, resistance poetry and narratives collaborate in liberation movements "alongside the gun, the pamphlet and the diplomatic delegation."[37] Harlow distinguishes between resistance poetry and narrative in regard to temporality. She claims that the poetry of organized resistance movements problematizes the given historical moment and the cultural images that underlie collective struggle. In contrast, resistance narrative examines the past, in particular the symbolic heritage with an eye to possible futures. In this sense, resistance narratives battle for that space to engage in the rewriting of history and, in the case of Angola, to imagine the basis for nationness. Moreover, Harlow's distinction between resistance poetry and narrative is important, especially in regard to the particular role that literature played in the Angolan nationalist struggle.

The contemporary phase of Angolan resistance literature began with poetry, as one might expect from Harlow's analysis. Poetry became the discursive space where Angolan writers sought to engage in immediate acts of cultural resistance focused on circumstances and events of the present condition. Acts of momentary resistance, however, necessarily require the consideration of what should be central to the formation of collective struggle. As previously discussed, the 1950s poetry moves people marginalized within the colonial formation to the discursive center where their voices and aspirations can be imagined. Resistance narratives also engage in imagining moments of resistance, but their length and complexity permit the textualizations of collective histories and futures.

Luandino Vieira's 1957 poem "Canção para Luanda" (Song for Luanda) poses the question, "Where is Luanda?"[38] The question is that of a temporary condition reinforced with the use of the verb *estar* (to be at the moment) rather than the expected and grammatically correct *ser* (to be as a permanent condition). The poetic voice is seeking the lost identity that formed the collective basis of a creolized past, which has been displaced by the tractors and settlers that have made Luanda a Europeanized city. The voices of the street vendor, the prostitute, the fishmonger, and others join together to answer that the other Luanda, that which has been covered with asphalt, remains in their hearts and collective consciousness. What the poem does not show is what that other Luanda was as the site of hybrid identity and resistance and what it might become in the imaginary constructs of nation. That more complex imagining, as will be discussed in chapter 2, completely dominates Luandino Vieira's resistance narratives written throughout the period of the protracted liberation struggle.

Luandino's narrative efforts to link invented pasts, presents, and futures is in reality the task of imagining a nation. In the colonial experience, the cultural imagining of what independence might be necessarily precedes the establishment of political independence itself. Independence once achieved, though, may require reimagining, as the nation imagined during resistance becomes the nation that functions or disintegrates after liberation.

In the case of Angola, moreover, the textual imagining of nation as an act of cultural resistance itself passed through various stages before independence. The length and complexities of the armed liberation struggle forced militant writers to abandon early didactic visions of nation as a culturally homogenous and socialist paradise. *Muana Puó*, the allegorical narrative of the creation of a utopian egalitarian society, is written by the same Pepetela who only a few years later reimagines a tense hybrid nation from within the guerrilla outpost of *Mayombe*. Luandino's early text, *Vidas Novas* (New Lives), optimistically imagines that the liberation struggle itself will transform the lives of common people, turning them from victims of the colonial order to liberated actors within the collective drama of creating nation. His later novel, *Nós, os do Makulusu* (We, Those from Makulusu), questions any such transformations and whether the collective "we" of the title might even survive the liberation struggle itself.

The very complexity of resistance, liberation, and independence in Angola precludes any accompanying narratives from imagining facile reconciliations within the projected postcolonial nation or, for that matter, within the transition itself from colony to nation. The dangers of the so-called liberating condition of postcolonialism that Ella Shohat convincingly critiques in "Notes on the Post-Colonial" include the uncomplicated construction of hybrid identity. As Shohat points out, and of particular relevance to the case of Angola, imperial powers also imagined hybrid identities and in fact justified colonialism itself as a hybridizing mission.[39] However, the acculturated identities that imperial Europe imagined can easily be mirrored in a simplistic countervision of the colonized, so that both imperial and revolutionary nationness might be conceived as ultimately the same. This colonial leveling of difference that was attempted through imperial policies of assimilation finds its counterpart in Benedict Anderson's often globalizing construct of nation as imagined community.[40] Anderson proposes not only that all modern nations imagine themselves as utopian constructs but also that they do so in the specific chronological order of European development. Thus all imagined communities are seen as emerging in a prescribed schematic fashion that echoes the very imaginings of imperial civilizing projects themselves.

The various constructs of a hybrid Angolan identity undertaken by the writers included in this book do not mirror the metropolitan constructs of pan-Lusitanian identity, nor do they, in the end, participate in envisioning a utopian nation. Homi Bhabha's description of hybridity as neither synthesis nor dialectics but rather as a disturbingly ambiguous liminal state of tension between colony and imagined nation-space provides the starting point for an analysis of narrations of nation in contemporary Angola.[41] That liminal space is the site of continued negotiations of hybridity that have emerged in the textualizations of Angolan nationness. Race, class, gender, ethnicity, tribe, region, generation—all play shifting roles in these negotiations, not only between narrative characters but also within the particular imagined Angolans themselves. In Fanon's phrasing, this often violent negotiation counters the colonial obsessions with classifications of subject in the imperial Manichaean imagined community.[42]

This negotiation of cultural hybridity gains further significance if we view it as an integral part of the processes of transculturation. Transculturation itself is a type of hybridization process on an abstract level. The negotiation of cultural identity described in these narratives shows that process being worked out, both as a negotiation of individual identities and as a negotiation of differences of national selfhood in the emerging nation. Moreover, if as Bhabha contends, cultural hybridity is negotiated in interstitial or liminal spaces that "entertain difference without an assumed or imposed hierarchy,"[43] then intersections of race, class, gender, tribe, region, and ethnicity in Angolan narratives also invite the reader to engage in the imaginings of a future hybrid nation.

National liberation in Angola was indeed an act of culture, a reclaiming of that terrain reserved for the colonizing subject that moved the marginalized perspective of the colonized to the center of a new nation-space. Once the periphery became the center, however, the identification of national subjects did not end with political independence. That ongoing negotiation, too, is an act of culture that ruptures the false and neocolonial boundary between colonialism and postcolonialism. Moreover, this boundary is that which appears to separate colonial Angola from national space, but as the events of the past two decades in Angola and elsewhere have proven, the border between nation and colony remains precarious. The narrative textualizations of this uneasy liminal space may better be described as counternarratives of nation that disrupt the monolithic construct of nation as imagined community. In short, Angolan writers explored and textualized the borderlands between what Angola had been, was, and dreamed of becoming, to chart the negotiated terrain of imagined nation-space.

Chapter 2

Countermapping Luanda

The Other Luanda

Luandino Vieira is the adopted name of José Vieira Mateus da Graça, born in 1935 in Portugal and brought to Luanda as a small child by his parents, settlers in Angola. An activist with the MPLA, he was imprisoned by the Portuguese New State for eleven years (1961–72) and spent most of that time in the Tarrafal camp for political prisoners in Cape Verde. Luandino was released in 1972, but the conditions of his parole were that he live only in Lisbon. His writing done in prison (in Luanda and Tarrafal) was, for the most part, not published until the Portuguese New State fell in 1974. Following Angolan independence, Luandino held several posts, the most recent and extended being that of Secretary of the União dos Escritores Angolanos (Angolan Writers Union or UEA).

Perhaps the best known internationally of Angolan fiction writers, Luandino began his extended literary career in the mid-1950s when he was associated with the Luanda-based journal *Cultura*.[1] Like the other nationalist writers and intellectuals of the period, in his early writings he engages the question of Angolan identity and begins a search that dominates his literary practice during the next twenty years.

That search, as mentioned in chapter 1, is indicated in his 1957 poem "Canção para Luanda" (Song for Luanda), which poses the question, "Where is Luanda?" Beyond evoking a specific Luanda, one that is being transformed by the post–World War II influx of Portuguese settlers to Africa, this questioning encompasses a search for a collective identity. The poem's vision of unity is strengthened by the use of a shared, creolized language and the evocation of a past cultural tradition that is assumed to be hybrid.

The imagining of that other Luanda as the heart of collective cultural identity forms the central problem of Luandino's prose fiction. Although the textualizations of a counter-Luanda rooted in collectivity presume a city that is currently Europeanized and divided, they are never undertaken from a colonial Manichaean position that celebrates the categorization of the colonized other. In Luandino's narratives, there is no easy separation between colonizer and colonized; rather, his countermappings of Luanda chart the fluid borders of hybridity in the colonized past, the revolutionary present, and the future nation.

These visions of hybridity and the rejection of a facile conjuring of Angolan identity introduce a new complexity to Angolan fiction. As discussed in the previous chapter, texts by earlier Angolan writers, such as António Assis Júnior's *O Segredo da Morta*, (The dead woman's secret), originally published in 1935, revindicate African cultural traditions but by assuming an ambiguous we/they position. A more recent example is Geraldo Bessa Victor's 1967 short story collection, *Sanzala sem Batuque* (Village without drums), which views Luanda's sociocultural transformations from an assimilated perspective of cultural superiority. As Russell Hamilton notes in *Voices from an Empire*, Bessa Victor may mourn the disappearance of African traditions, but he ultimately sees their passing as a benefit to the Portuguese patriarchy with which he himself identifies.[2]

For Luandino Vieira, Luanda is imagined as the matrix of cultural collectivity precisely at the moment of radical displacement. The other Luanda of the past is one in which creolized cultural practices had emerged, in part, as a result of the limited Portuguese settler presence. The New State's intensified efforts to transform Angola into a white settler colony not only upset Luanda's demographic patterns but also the patterns of creolization. Socioeconomic and racial distinctions manifested in the division of a creolized Luanda into African and European sectors. In *Angola under the Portuguese*, Gerald Bender describes the impact of the intense settler influx into Luanda in terms of a growing white city that expanded into the borders of African neighborhoods and in some cases overran established sections of the city.[3]

This displacement figures prominently in 1950s narratives that concentrated on the sociocultural contradictions of colonial urban society. These urban-based works, whether those by Arnaldo Santos that assumed a *crónica* (chronicle) form or others by Mário António that were more intimist, read as *quadros sociais* (social portraits) of contemporary *luandense* society. Luandino Vieira's early narratives share in this critical representation of colonial society, particularly in terms of the fragmentation of imagined collectivity.

Critics of Luandino's prose fiction generally ascertain the development of his literary production in terms of the ruptures produced by certain of the works. Salvato Trigo, for instance, in his book-length study, *Luandino Vieira o Logoteta*, identifies two distinct phases in Luandino's literary production with *Luuanda* (1964) as the text that marks the rupture. For Trigo, this rupture is understood in terms of discontinuity, so that in the first phase Luandino writes to narrate, while in the second, he narrates to write.[4] The early texts, therefore, are characterized by the immediacy of representation, while those written after *Luuanda* emphasize the process of textual production itself.

In an interesting counter to Trigo's demarcation, José Ornelas admits a certain decentralization of representation but with the provision that Luandino's texts always return to the representative.[5] I would add that this return is what creates a single literary project whose focus is that of remapping the contours of Luanda's hybrid identity. Moreover, as Stuart Hall reminds us, the narrated invention of identity is that which is "never complete, always in process, and always constituted within . . . representation."[6] For Luandino Vieira, this process of inventing identity is a continuing project that, of course, changes over time and becomes increasingly concerned with how to represent hybridity within narrative discourse.

It is not surprising that critics such as Trigo understand this project to be ones of ruptures, since what is really at stake is a battle for both subjectivity and discursive terrain. What are perceived as ruptures are actually violent negotiations of hybridity to define the liminal space that can be claimed as Angolan narrative. That space of liminality, I would argue, is that of the transculturated *estória* in which the narratives themselves are as difficult to categorize as the imaginings of Luanda (see chapter 4). It is a charting of narrative space, moreover, that begins with Luandino Vieira's earliest works, in which, as the author himself claims, "Everything is already there."[7]

Transculturation and the Hybrid *Estória*

A Cidade e a Infância (The city and childhood), originally published in 1960 by the Casa dos Estudantes do Império, represents the first book-length collection of prose fiction by a writer associated with the 1950s literary-cultural groups. In 1957, Luandino Vieira attempted to publish a different group of stories under the same title. The edition, which was to be published by Cadernos Nzambi in Luanda, was confiscated from the typesetter. The 1957 *caderno* (booklet) contained four stories, only one of which, "Encontro de Acaso" (Chance meeting), is included in the 1960 edition.

Critics of *A Cidade e a Infância* often recognize it as a prefiguration of Luandino Vieira's subsequent narrative fiction. Salvato Trigo, for example, describes this collection as the antetext of practically all of Luandino's writings.[8] Russell Hamilton contends not only that the stories are hymns to the creole-African city, but that they also contain the beginnings of techniques and discourses that later will characterize Luandino Vieira as the storyteller-griot of Luanda.[9] The ten stories in A Cidade e a Infância are arranged according to the dates of production (1954–57), but this arrangement also indicates a shift in the narrative focus that moves from the fragmentation of luandense identity to the emergence of a new identity initially voiced through protests against conditions in the colonial city.

This fragmentation of imagined collectivity dominates the first five stories of A Cidade e a Infância and is represented through the alienated positions of the narrators and/or characters from the always problematic but often idealized hybrid past. The opening story, "Encontro de Acaso," for example, recounts the chance meeting between two childhood friends from the Luanda neighborhood of Kinaxixi. This story is characteristic of the concern in the early narratives with the breakdown of imagined collectivity. The "we" of the interracial Kinaxixi group has been divided, like the increasingly Europeanized Luanda itself, into the "I" of the white narrator and the "he" of the black friend who has become marginalized within the transforming city. Kinaxixi has been destroyed by the instruments of European urbanization as the narrator says, "Envious tractors going after bands of unknown enemies invaded our forest and tore down the trees."[10]

The collectivity of the creolized city and childhood is reimagined in "Encontro de Acaso" through the harmonica music coming from a bar. For the narrator, the music becomes the song "of all of us, young black and white boys who ate sweets and fried fish, who made escapes and slingshots, and who on rainy mornings laid down our dirty body in the dirty water and with a well cleansed soul went to conquer the fortress from the Kinaxixi bandits."[11] Here the reimagined collectivity serves a dual purpose: it bridges the alienated position between the narrator and his childhood friend, again united in the "we" of the past, and it negotiates the space between past and present within a narrative that permits the recuperation, however tenuous and invented, of hybrid collectivity. Luandino's 1972 estória, "Kinaxixi Kiami!," also depicts the destructiveness of the Europeanization of Luanda. In this story, Lourentinho is imprisoned for running down an engineer with a tractor rather than obey his command to tear down a sacred mulemba tree. Lourentinho's protest, of course, is the refusal to participate in the destruction of Kinaxixi. Moreover, the Kinaxixi that he reimagines—the title in Kimbundo means "My Kinaxixi!"—is forever the center of new dreams.[12]

"Encontro de Acaso," like several other stories, imagines a specific childhood that has been dissipated in the divided city. Colonial-style urbanization not only bulldozed the *musseques* but also that shared childhood of tense collectivity. This destruction informs "A Fronteira de Asfalto" (The asphalt frontier), in which the pavement marks the separation between past and present as well as the racial boundary in a divided, colonial Luanda. In this story, a black young man named Ricardo and a white teenage girl question the imposed breakdown of their friendship, but, as Ricardo insists, that relationship was always conditioned by the racist ideology of colonialism: "When I was your friend Ricardo, a clean and polite little black boy, like your mother used to say."[13] As Manuel Ferreira emphasizes in his preface to the collection's second edition, certain conditions of Portuguese colonialism permitted a limited racial coexistence in the Luanda of the past that has been destroyed by the hegemonical practices of the New State, thus creating an asphalt frontier.[14] The pavement, however, simply places a clear marker on what was always there, so that when Ricardo reiterates that the illusion remains in the past, he refers to the illusion of collectivity always contained within the boundaries of colonialism.

The narrations of past collectivity become increasingly complex in the first half of *A Cidade e a Infância*, culminating in the fragmented discourse of the title story, a stream-of-consciousness narration of Zito, the son of white settlers. The final narrative fragment of this story indicates a total displacement from the past, so that Zito's memories, once vivid, are reduced to distorted images in a picture-postcard city. This dislocation of the past is also a disarticulation that emphasizes the fragmentation of the narrative segments. The unity imposed by the associative evocations is ruptured at the closing; although a final fragment of the past remains, it appears as a diluted and meaningless image.

The second group of stories in *A Cidade e a Infância* moves to a questioning of the unjust socioeconomic relations of the colonial formation. This questioning is voiced by the characters and narrators in a prefiguration of the revolt that marks Luandino Vieira's later collection of prose, *Vidas Novas* (New lives), written in 1962. The protest, and in some cases incipient revolt, are directed against the exploitation of the colonized, but they do not move beyond the questioning negation of colonial identity to assume a collective Angolan one, as is the case of *Vidas Novas* and *A Vida Verdadeira de Domingos Xavier* (The real life of Domingos Xavier), both written after the 1961 outbreak of armed nationalist conflict.

Some of the stories do propose a relationship between storytelling and the emerging sociopolitical protest. In "Bebiana," Don'Ana, the teller of "old folks' stories," relates her life story as a *quitandeira* and her relationship with a Portuguese merchant in order to convince the narrator to marry her mulatto daughter, Bebiana. Her story ultimately provokes the white narrator to question his own motives as well as those of Bebiana: does he perceive Bebiana as an exotic mixture of races, and does he represent for her one more step up in colonial society?

In "Companheiros," the only story set outside of Luanda (in what was then Nova Lisboa), one of the characters from the musseques of Luanda appears as a storyteller capable of transforming reality: "The life of the mulatto Armindo was sad! But when he told stories it seemed even beautiful. Just like those stories in the movies." [15] Armindo's stories also contribute to the transformation of his two companions, who assume an attitude of revolt when their friend is picked up by the colonial police. Here the actual process of storytelling has the possibility to create new identities of resistance, if only at the level of imagination. Storytelling itself becomes an act of resistance.

In this vein, "Faustino" employs a narrative voice that clearly prefigures the narrator-griot of Luandino Vieira's later estórias. The story begins and ends with variations of a formula-like technique of orature: "Now I will tell the story of Faustino. Don'Ana didn't tell it to me, no sir. I saw this story myself, another part he himself told me." [16] An intertextual relationship is established between "Bebiana" and "Faustino" with particular relevance to the role of the storyteller. The narrator of "Faustino" assumes Don'Ana's role in order to recount the story of protest. Don'Ana clearly presents the stories of the past, and though her stories are meaningful in the present, she remains distanced from that present. The narrator takes over this role as the storyteller of the present—and thus situates himself within an awareness of colonial contradictions—to relate the story of Faustino, whose revolt is provoked by the desire to study. A sense of narrative immediacy prevails through the use of the formulaic opening and closing, in which the act of storytelling seemingly is directed toward an imagined audience. "Faustino" represents the first instance in Luandino Vieira's literary practice in which oral storytelling techniques are incorporated into the written narrative. Although this narrative still appears in the form of an *história* (story), "Faustino" prefigures the more fully elaborated estórias of radical negotiations in *Luuanda*.

This formula-like construction appears again in several stories included in *Vidas Novas*.[17] This collection, as its title indicates, textualizes the transformations of imagined Angolans through the revolutionary struggle. Though somewhat didactic, the narratives propose a relation between storytelling and subjectivity as a means to elaborate types of collective identity. This is evident in "Cardoso Kamukolo, Sapateiro" (Cardoso Kamukolo, shoemaker), an exemplary tale of sacrifice and solidarity that assumes the form of a narrative within a narrative.[18] This multilayered story begins with the voice of a contemporary narrator who imagines a second storyteller in a future independent Angola. For the first time, the term "estória" describes the storytelling process in a proximation of oral and literary narratives as transculturated practice. The grandfather, the storyteller of the future, begins his story of Cardoso Kamukolo with a formulaic opening: "So, now I will put the story of Job Maukuaja of the Cuanhama people, and of his friend Mário João." [19]

The use of the verb *pôr* (to put), which later appears extensively in Luandino Vieira's estórias, instead of the traditional Portuguese *contar* (to tell), corresponds directly to the opening of the Kimbundu tale, or *missosso*.[20] Furthermore, in "Cardoso Kamukolo, Sapateiro," the term "estória" appears in relation to both the story of Cardoso Kamukolo, who dies while defending a child from a white vigilante mob, and the traditional tales, described by the grandfather as "estórias of our people." Clearly, the exemplary story of Cardoso Kamukolo also pertains to a collective culture of the imagined future, as a hybrid form of Angolan narrative.

Luuanda, like *Vidas Novas*, was written in the Cadeia Central da Pide in Luanda and received the top Angolan literary prize in 1964. The following year, a jury composed of Portuguese writers and critics awarded *Luuanda* the highest award for fiction from the Portuguese Writers Society. In the controversy surrounding the decision to bestow that literary honor on a work whose author was imprisoned for political activities against the New State, the Portuguese government disbanded the society, and several members of the jury were interrogated and held by the PIDE, the Portuguese secret police. *Luuanda* was revised by the author in 1972 and published by Edições 70. Marcelo Caetano's government confiscated the edition and fined the publisher. One more edition should be noted, a 1965 illegal edition indicating that it was published in Brazil. It was actually published by PIDE agents in Braga, Portugal, in an attempt to obtain money.

Luuanda[21] represents Luandino Vieira's first elaborated use of the estória form with two of the three narratives—"Estória da Galinha e do Ovo" (The tale of the hen and the egg) and "Estória do Ladrão e do Papagaio" (The tale of the thief and the parrot)—containing "estória" in their titles. In *Luuanda*, "estória" designates the transculturated narrative form that incorporates oral storytelling techniques of the Kimbundu missosso. During an interview with Luandino Vieira, he told of first encountering the term in a footnote by ethnologist Lopes Cardoso that differentiated between "estória" and "história." Luandino further elaborated on the written estória as the textualization of the *estória oral*: "That is, it can be told by another person and maintain a thread that identifies it, so that each person can do variations."[22] This open form of the estória finds it roots in the traditional missosso, in which the formulaic Kimbundu opening—"eme ngateletele"—employs the iterative form of the verb *ku-ta*. This verb translates into the Portuguese as "pôr," (to put), but in this context actually means "to put various times."[23] Luandino Vieira underscored the repetitive basis of the estória as "something that was told and that now I am telling and that will be told again."[24]

In *Luuanda*, the open form of the estória is most explicit in "Estória do Ladrão e do Papagaio." Here the narrator-griot addresses the specific problem of how to "pôr a estória" (put the story). The metatextual commentary begins in the voice of one of the characters, Xico Futa, who attempts to discern the real cause of Garrido Fernandes' arrest: "The parrot Jacó, old and sick, was stolen by a lame mulatto, Garrido Fernandes, shy of women because of his foot, and nicknamed Kam'tuta. But where does the tale begin?" [25] This central question triggers an extended analogy with the cashew tree that maintains its *fio de vida* (thread of life) despite repeated attempts to destroy it.

Clearly, this narrative segment on the extensive and indestructible roots of the tree presents a reflection on how to discern the root of the estória: "A beginning must be chosen: it usually begins, because it's easier, with the root of the tree, with the root of things, with the root of events, of arguments."[26] Following the recounting of the parable, the narrative voice then resumes the search for the roots of the estória: "Now then, we can talk about the root of the affair of the arrest of Kam'tuta as being Jacó, the bad-mannered parrot, although further back we're going to meet Inácia, the nice plump girl he loved even though she was short on affection; and ahead Dosreis and João Miguel, people who didn't pay him much attention and laughed at those ideas of a lame boy."[27]

The metatextual commentary on how to form the estória indicates the multiple roots or stories that inform each particular narration. In this version, the narrator chooses the parrot Jacó as the root. The estória, however, is a convergence of stories—in this case at least those of Garrido, Inácia, João Miguel, and Dosreis. A different narration or selection of another root or beginning would result in another version of the same estória. Luandino Vieira's literary incorporation of the missosso emphasizes the open and repetitive characteristics of orature that are defined not through duplication but through narrative variation. The roots of the estória are interwoven, but they eventually surface, with more or less narrative emphasis, in the possible narrations.

This open characteristic of the estória is less evident in "Estória da Galinha e do Ovo," but here too the narrator, as Russell Hamilton explains, assumes the role of a griot who elaborates his tale within molds and formulas transformed from orality.[28] The particular oral context in this estória is that of the

Kimbundu *maka*, described by ethnographer Héli Chatelain as revolving around the question of who is right or wrong. In all the maka, the chief protagonists are either exonerated or found guilty by what they do or say. Some of the maka contain lawsuits with pleadings by both sides to determine the correct judgment.[29]

The particular maka of "Estória da Galinha e do Ovo" centers on the dispute between two musseque neighbors who claim an egg laid by the hen of one in the other's yard. Five additional characters are summoned to judge the case: Bebeca, the *mais-velha* (the elder wise woman) of the musseque; Só Zé, a white shopkeeper; Azulinho, a seminary student; Só Vitalinho, the musseque landlord; and Só Lemos, a former notary assistant. Clearly, the judges represent various elements of the colonial social formation—the commercial class, the clergy, the property owner, and the judicial system—all of which conspire against the people's interests in the text. Furthermore, and in relation to the multiple roots of the estória, each character's story is included in the narration. In this sense, although the maka itself remains the central narrative focus, the estória maintains its plural form.

This plural and open form here extends to include the collectivity of reception. "Estória da Galinha e do Ovo" ends with the narrator's exhortation to the readers: "My tale. If it's pretty, if it's ugly, only you know. But I swear I didn't tell a lie and that these affairs happened in this our land of Luanda."[30] As Russell Hamilton emphasizes, this closing indicates a movement from the particular to the collective while designating yet another judicial role to the audience.[31] In this instance the readers are invited to judge not only *estes casos* (these arguments) but also the estória itself.

Luandino's elaboration of the transculturated estória in *Luuanda* represents a decisive pass in the retaking of discursive terrain reserved for purely acculturated discourse. By indicating the hybrid estória as that vehicle for textualizing collective identity, his narrations open the margins of the written text to practices of orature within traditional Kimbundu culture. The transculturated narratives, as hybrid forms of imagining Luanda, turn to that other city, in this case the Kimbundu Luuanda of the title. Here is an Africanized terrain that is the countermapping to the divided colonial city of *A Cidade e a Infância*. The constructs of identity, like those of the estórias themselves, are replete with the possibilities of many roots, many arguments, and many future narrations. And although the author signs off on the written tale, these textualizations of hybrid identity are posited as collective narrations of "our land of Luanda."

The estória as hybrid narrative is further developed in *Velhas Estórias* (Old stories), whose narrations were first conceived during the same period as

Luuanda but were revised between 1965 and 1966 following Luandino Vieira's transfer from Luanda to the Tarrafal prison camp in the Cape Verdean archipelago. Luandino Vieira specifically refers to this period between the writing of *Luuanda* and the 1967 novel, *Nós, os do Makulusu* as one of literary meditation concerning the paths his narratives had taken in the estórias of *Luuanda*.[32] *Velhas Estórias*, finished during this period of reflection, bridges the metatextual questionings of *Luuanda* and the radical resistance narration of the 1967 novel. These four estórias also demonstrate a further experimentation with the open and plural form of the hybrid text, as well as with the interpolative role of the narrator-griot.

As was the case with *Luuanda*'s estórias, the telling of "A Estória da Menina Santa" (The story of the young girl, Santa) revolves around sorting out the multiple narrative threads. The estória of Santa's pregnancy incorporates the stories of the Portuguese merchant António Júlio dos Santos, how he became Julinho Kanini, and his arrest on charges of diamond smuggling, all within the story of the expansion of the Makutu musseque. The narrative movement recalls "Estória do Ladrão e do Papagaio" as the storyteller begins the tale with a beginning that is not the actual root of the estória. Observations on how to produce the estória once again begin with the questioning voice of a character who compares life to a river of complex waters. The narrator expounds on this statement at length to initially conclude that "a river truly seems like the life of a person."[33] Here, however, the routes of the river open up to the possible roots of the estória: "Makutu, a river; the life of Kanini, also a river, rivers flowing together in the separate. . . . The rivers meet in the sea of many more waters."[34] The narrative search leads to a "beautiful confusion of waters"—the complications of other roots and stories. This specific narration is only one possibility within the plural estória form and does not preclude other potential narrations.

The production of the estória also forms a central focus of "O Último Quinzar do Makulusu" (The last *quinzar* of Makulusu), which, as Salvato Trigo points out, is reminiscent of "Cardoso Kamukolo, Sapateiro" and prefigures "Cangundos, Verdianos, San Tomistas, Nossa Gente" (Cangundos, Verdeans, San Tomistas, our people) as an "estória of an estória."[35] The narrator recounts how Sá Domingas knew many estórias that she had learned as a child from her parents, but that she never repeats her stories; instead she continually reinvents a tale that differs with each telling. Sa Domingas's estória of the quinzar—a half-human, half-animal monster of popular luandense folklore—ends with the same formula used by the narrator-griot of *Luuanda*'s estórias: "If my estória is pretty, if it is ugly, you're the ones who know."[36]

"O Último Quinzar do Makulusu," like two other tales in *Velhas Estórias*, takes place in the Luanda of the past. Luandino's literary return to the place in time, following the contemporary settings of *A Vida Verdadeira de Domingos Xavier*, *Vidas Novas*, and *Luuanda*, also marks a return to the narrative tension between the creolized childhood past and the colonized present that prevailed in *A Cidade e a Infância*. In "O Último Quinzar do Makulusu," the narrator opens the estória with a setting of the spatial-temporal context: "The arguments that I will put, took place on that forgotten night of March 11, 1938 in Makulusu, in those times our musseque."[37] The displacement is later revoiced at the close of the estória: "That was the last time that cases of the quinzar took place in Makulusu, in those times our musseque and today a white neighborhood."[38] This distancing between "our musseque" and the contemporary white neighborhood that stands in its place is countered by the storytelling process. The imagining of the hybrid but collective musseque as the site of resistance finds complex expression in the doubled narration of an estória within an estória.

The imagining of hybrid identity through the plural roots of the estória forms the basis of Luandino's long estória, *João Vêncio: Os Seus Amores* (written in 1968) in which the imprisoned João Vêncio tells his life stories to another prisoner.[39] Although the voice of the other prisoner does not appear in the written text, the "dialogue" is not one-sided; João Vêncio continually addresses, questions, and answers his interlocutor, so that the narration also is informed by its active reception. Luandino later employs a similar storytelling technique in "Kinaxixi Kiami," in which the imprisoned Lourentinho relates his own story to a fellow inmate. Both "Kinaxixi Kiami!" and *João Vêncio* recall the narrative strategies of Brazilian fiction writer João Guimarães Rosa, in particular in his monumental *Grande Sertão: Veredas*. Here Riobaldo's tells his story to an outsider from Brazil's urbanized coast who is taking notes and subsequently writing the story. In Luandino's works, the interlocutors take no less active a role in the storytelling process, and in *João Vêncio*, too, the interlocutor is writing down the story.

This narration, like many of Luandino's other estórias opens during a conversation between João Vêncio and the other prisoner: "This man asks the craziest questions! . . . You want to know why I'm in the lockup?"[40] The estória, of course, never achieves its form through singularity so that the interlocutor's question opens the narrative to the multiple levels that inform João Vêncio's seemingly simple story. Vêncio's imprisonment stems not only from the particular act of attempted homicide but rather from his cumulative life stories. The proposal to relate those stories to the other prisoner—"eu queria pôr para o senhoro minhas alíneas"—specifies a mixture of the narrative techniques of orature, with the formulaic use of "pôr," and of literature with "alíneas."

This combination of orature and literature also is evident in the pact that João Vêncio, the storyteller, proposes to his interlocutor, symbolized by their joint stringing of the beads of a *missanga* necklace: "I'll hold the thread while you, comrade, put on the beads, and little by little we'll make our necklace of commingled colors."[41] If João Vêncio is to relate his stories, the interlocutor's task is that of putting the missanga beads, or pieces, into an order. At several points, Vêncio interrupts his storytelling to emphasize their joint narrative venture and indicates that his comrade in prison is writing notes. Here the hybrid nature of the pact gains new importance as the oral string of stories is ordered by the written order of the missanga beads. João Vêncio may "pôr a estória," but it is the *muadié* (boss) who provides the alíneas. There is no evidence that the interlocutor has omitted or changed any of João Vêncio's associative and meandering oral narration, but his persistent (though unheard) questions and comments are incorporated and in that way determine the narrative order of the estória. The stringing of the missanga necklace not only represents the narrative's joint construction but also points to the plurality of the estória's discourse.

This plural character extends beyond the multiple stories and temporalities that comprise the narrative to encompass each textual fragment or case. The narration ends somewhat abruptly with Vêncio's sharp rebuttal to the interlocutor's final question: "This man asks the craziest questions! . . . Separate beads on the string—you think that's what a man's life is. Red beads, blue beads, this color, that color, all in a row? No, sir! . . . Everything a man does is all of him, whole—each and every color is the rainbow."[42] The narrative returns to the opening question ("This man asks the craziest questions") of the interlocutor, who, it appears, has failed after all to grasp Vêncio's claim that the simple case of his imprisonment must be told through his life's many stories. The missanga beads on the string are not his life, but rather the order provided by the muadié. As João Vêncio retorts, each story, each event that he has related is all of him and every single missanga bead has the colors of the rainbow. The educated interlocutor—and here "muadié" can be taken as a sign of class separation between the two prisoners, as it is sometimes understood as "boss"—strings the stories together but does not recognize in this singular necklace the potential others that might be made from the same beads.

While this failure to understand the dynamics of orality brings the joint narrative venture to a close, the estória itself does not end in failure if we think in terms of storytelling as resistance. João Vêncio is perhaps Luandino's ultimate imagined hybrid identity and, as will be discussed in the last section of this chapter, appropriates all the discourses of colonialism and transnational capitalism in the distinctive patois of a pimp, cicerone, and, of course, modern-day colonized and hybrid storyteller. Here in the colonial prison, João Vêncio passes the time of his imprisonment by stringing missanga beads and telling stories to the literate muadié. The latter may write what he believes to have heard, but ultimately, João Vêncio's oral estória is marked by what Doris Sommer has termed "the rhetoric of refusal." Sommer identifies as "resistant" those texts that ultimately withhold the secrets of communities from readers who, quite simply put, cannot know. In *João Vêncio: Os Seus Amores*, the muadié, as outsider, is incapable of knowing the multiplicity of the resistant self that João Vêncio presents in his oral narration. João Vêncio stops the estória short. His Kimbundu *kana ngana* ("no sir") resonates with the refusal of resistance as he keeps for himself the many meanings of his estória. The muadié may walk away from the prison with notebook in hand, or more likely pieces of torn paper, but that which belongs to the resistant textualization of Vêncio's life has been refused him. Here, of course, the storyteller's name takes on added significance. Vêncio may be imprisoned, but he is not defeated, for within the domain of his storytelling he proves victorious against those who might appropriate his tale and ultimately his life's meaning as hybridity.

It is this very sense of the resistance of the hybrid, transculturated narrative that marks the estórias collected in *Macandumba*, published in 1978. *Macandumba* returns to Luanda in the time of *Luuanda*, so that its opening epigraph—"Jikul'o mesu! Uala mu Luuanda" (Open your eyes! You're in Luanda)—serves as a warning not only to the characters to beware the violent and potentially deadly context but also to the readers—those who might understand—to be aware of the text.

This double-edged warning indeed pertains to "Cangundos, Verdianos, Santomistas, Nossa Gente," another of Luandino's estórias within an estória. This particular text opens with the creolized Kimbundu-Portuguese lyrics of a song attributed to the musical group Ritmo Iaxikelela.[43] As Russell Hamilton indicates, "Whoever understands the meaning of the song . . . is already in the plot of the estória."[44] The song itself represents the key to the mystery of a counterfeit lottery ticket, but the solution is open only to those who understand the creolized luandense lyrics. Among the police, only Justiniano— *filho-de-país*—with his *experiência luandista* (born in Angola with Luandan experience) finally decodes the solution provided by the song.

The narrator-griot jumps right into the confusion of the arguments to in-terpret the order of the estória: "Arguments that are in the song, are those that are most confused—the musseque poet is always the only boss of his very different truths."[45] Right from the start we are informed that the song is sub-ject to the rules of musseque poetics as the narrator establishes the order of the estória through an interpretation of the lyrics: "Look, in the song they put: 'The colonist went to jail' or in official Portuguese: 'The policeman gave entry into the underground prison.' Musseque exaggerations, you'll see very soon, the estorias' lessons will show you."[46] The narrator's translation of the hybrid lyrics into "state Portuguese" counters this dominating discourse of colonization while revealing only part of the song's secrets.

The narrative movement also is marked by the repeated references to a game played by musseque children: "It's like this, in cases with whites in-volved, everything seems like the game of musseque children: hill of red sand, there inside a string carelessly rolled; if you pull it, slowly, slowly, the matches sticking in there will fall."[47] As the narration progresses, the estória opens to the complex interweaving of the characters' stories—including the Cape Verdean, Robertom, the santomense (or "santomista"), Alceu, and Evu, origi-nally from Porto—who, as in the musseque game, fall into the trap when the thread of the estória is slowly pulled.

The different stories of the Sambizanga dwellers not only combine to form the estória but also voice the hybridity of the *luandense musseque*. Robertom's *terra-longismo*—the longing for his Cape Verdean birthplace—Alceu and Marília's pretentious mestizo aspirations and Evu's socialization into musseque culture all converge within the estória of the counterfeit lottery ticket. This is, after all, Luuanda.

Luanda is also the setting of "Pedro Caliota, Sapateiro Andante," in which all the storytelling paths are inverted.[48] The estória begins with Caliota's at-tempt to buy back the fish that he had sold earlier in the day. The narration, however, is in reverse sequence until it reaches its true beginning or root— the discovery of a five-hundred *escudo* bill in the belly of Caliota's last fish. The plural form of the estória emerges not only through Pedro Caliota's vari-ous encounters as he meanders through Luanda—for the people he meets each have their own estórias, to be sure—but also through the three ques-tions raised by the narrator-griot. The first appears at the beginning of the estória: "In order to be able to put the estória, first one must ask: the same— Pedro Caliota, in white ignorance assimilated as Iscariotes—who wanted to make a viola from a tail, to put forth some cases that took place in a missosso estória, in the long ago?"[49] This question opens one level of the estória—

Pedro Caliota's careless and carefree wanderings through Luanda and his ingenuous belief in the innate benevolence of people and the good fortune of life's events. The remaining questions end the estória and indicate not only two other levels but also other possible estórias: "Returning to the arguments: Caliota, poor Peter or Moses dead in the waters, whoever could have thought that they were immortal in '61? . . . But to begin another estória I want to know: can a person die, be badly murdered and dead on a day of all suns?"[50] This second question sets the immediate context of the estória as the 1961 outbreak of armed conflict in Luanda. Caliota, whatever he is called, has not heeded the context and dies at the hands of Portuguese vigilantes. The final question lifts the estória from its very violent context and questions the injustice of death—anyone's death—in the face of nature's beauty on that day of all suns.

These three questions, moreover, point to the very hybridity of the transculturated estória as central to Luandino Vieira's project of narrative resistance. The first question indicates the meanderings of orature, an associative practice that resists the rigid boundaries of the written text, but within the context of Luandino's writings allows a certain fluidity, though never carelessness, to the fixed limits of the monolingual histories of the colonizers. The very possibilities of those meanderings introduce other potential polyglot estórias in a transculturated practice that itself is both hybrid and revolutionary. The second question is contextual and situates the resistant texts in a revolutionary Luanda as a privileged imagined space of violence and counterviolence that is precisely that moment of affirmation of complex hybrid identities. The narrator's final question is that which lifts the estória to an imagined future in which those other estórias might be realized in less violent postrevolutionary contexts.

Luandino's estórias imagine the boundaries of Luanda, that other city, in a countermapping to the Europeanized colonial terrain. If the official map of Luanda has rigid frontiers of race, temporality, and class, all expressed in European narrative forms, the countermap of Luandino's hybrid terrain textualizes a city with indeterminate borderlands but not fixed boundaries. These borderlands are the very liminal narrative sites that engage the possibilities of revolutionary change in a form of narration that is itself fluid, plural, and open.

Resistance Novels: Textualizations of the Collective "We"

Luandino Vieira's two novels—A Vida Verdadeira de Domingos Xavier (written in 1961) and Nós, os do Makulusu (written in 1967)—also demonstrate the fluidity and plurality of the non-fixed estórias. These are not tales of imagined collectivity to be recounted in possible future contexts but rather resistance narratives in the sense that Edward Said puts forth in *Culture and Imperialism*. For Said, resistance is understood in part not only as a contestation to imperialism but more importantly "as an alternative way of conceiving human history."[51] In this sense both novels, though quite different from each other, elaborate invented collective histories that are integral in their plurality and perhaps even somewhat utopic in their search for different historical endings.

The difference between the two narratives resides more specifically in their positions within the revolutionary struggle in Angola. *A Vida Verdadeira de Domingos Xavier*, written in the first year of the nationalist conflict, is an immediate textualization of resistance and collective identity. *Nós, os do Makulusu*, written from prison six years into the nationalist war, opens up the imagined collectivity of the hybrid Luanda to a radical reconfiguration of the symbols and images that sustained the creolized city. Both texts, as Barbara Harlow proposes in her work on resistance novels, analyze the dominant relations of power albeit within the specific revolutionary moments of rupture that expose those very power structures.[52] Moreover, as resistance novels Luandino's works are set in the revolutionary present but imagine an integral past that opens up the possible futures.

Figurations of collective identity, resistance, and revolt dominate the various narrative levels in *A Vida Verdadeira de Domingos Xavier*, written during Luandino's stay in Portugal in late 1961. He completed the manuscript only days prior to his arrest and subsequent deportation to Luanda. Although an official edition was not published until 1974, copies of the original manuscript were circulated prior to that date.[53]

The novel's title provokes expectations of the literary biography or even exposé—the real life—of one character. In actuality, *A Vida Verdadeira de Domingos Xavier* is composed of several narratives and discursive temporalities that are all unified by a single narrative event, the imprisonment of Domingos Xavier. This interweaving of stories provides an integrating perspective of the unifying narrative event and also textualizes the different levels of resistance against the colonial regime. This composite vision of the collective struggle forms the true focus of *A Vida Verdadeira de Domingos Xavier* and as such is the novel's real protagonist.

Luandino has stated that the novel's popularity is due to its relative narrative accessibility and linear movement.[54] Actually the chapters are not ordered chronologically, and, as Pires Laranjeira points out, the novel is marked by a "rupture of the linear" within the individual chapters themselves.[55] The first three chapters establish the three major story lines: the activities of the organized nationalist movement in Luanda, Maria's search for her husband, and Domingos Xavier's imprisonment, torture, and death. The narrative perspective also switches constantly so that although the ninth chapter concerns Maria's search, her actions are seen through the eyes of Zito and Petela. The meaning of the narrative resides in the conjuncture of these stories; the novel's vision of collectivity depends upon this plurality.

The collective basis of resistance and struggle is established within each of the stories. This appears most evident in the narration of the militant clandestine movement in Luanda. In his preface to the French translation published in 1971, three years before the novel's publication in Portuguese, Mário Pinto de Andrade describes the text as a sociological painting of resistance and adds that "the narrative of Domingos Xavier's life does not only permit one to understand the degree of mobilization and of the integration of social classes in the nationalist combat, but also clarifies, through diverse dialogues, its nature and its content."[56] The actions of the nationalist movement center on deciphering a mystery—the identity of the prisoner brought to Luanda. These actions follow an established trajectory from the child, Zito, to Petela to Xico to Miguel to Mussunda, all of whom are united in the last chapter. The inclusion of Mussunda and other historical figures such as Carlos Vieira Dias ("Liceu") further situates the narrative within the immediacy of the liberation struggle.[57] The novel—written shortly after the February 1961 MPLA attack in Luanda that initiated the outbreak of nationalist conflict—identifies with the immediacy of that struggle, which underlies the urgency of the text.

Domingos Xavier's own story is prototypic and, as Maria Lúcia Lepecki explains, might represent the portrait of "any fighter or of any patriot who lives in analogous circumstances."[58] His story assumes representative stature in its treatment of the heroic resistance of a common man and his subsequent transformation into a symbol of Angolan resistance. The real emphasis, however, is on collective rather than individual struggle. Furthermore, this textualization of collectivity focuses on daily oppression and, of course, on day-to-day resistance. Domingos Xavier's torture and death, Maria's persistent search in the police headquarters of the colonial regime, the resistance of the musseque dwellers, and the actions of the militants in the nationalist movement are all representative of the various levels and forms of imagined collectivity in the novel.

The narrative voice itself is not impartial but rather forms part of this collective resistance as it dialogues with the prisoner to offer encouragement: "Your friends know that you are imprisoned and trust in you, they send you notes with words of courage, you must get through this, Domingos Xavier. It's true, brothers, I must get through this."[59] In the final chapter, as members of the Ngola Ritmos band are about to perform, the narrator speaks directly to the imprisoned Liceu: "True, brother Liceu, true. You still haven't reached the end, we are all with you in your prison. Ngola plays your music, the people don't forget, brother Liceu."[60] In both of these instances, the narrator speaks with the unity of imagined Angolan peoples (*irmãos*, *povo*) and opens the discourse to a voice that represents the collective.

More important, it is precisely in this vision of collectivity that the biographical expectations of European narratives are countered in a life story that is anything but singular. In this sense, the novel appears more as a counternarrative to acculturated discourse as it establishes the real life of Domingos Xavier in the heart of an imagined Angolan people. Here the text echoes the answer to the question first posed in Luandino's 1957 poem. Luanda, after all, was always in the collective heart of its people. And in the 1961 novel, the search to determine the truth of Domingos Xavier's arrest takes the various characters through Luanda with its many networks of resistance that remain invisible to those outside of the community. Maria's questions as to her husband's whereabouts may go unanswered at the different colonial headquarters, but the real answers reside in the support of the people she encounters in the musseques. Finally, *A Vida Verdadeira de Domingos Xavier* imagines a collective symbolic reclaiming of the body of the tortured prisoner that parallels the reclaiming of the colonized city under the very eyes of the Portuguese authorities. His true life becomes part of the communal memory of Angolans bound together not only in colonialism but also in the imagined visions of resistance.

Written from the prison in Tarrafal, *Nós, os do Makulusu* questions the very survival of both communal memory and collectivity within the violent ruptures of the Angolan liberation struggle. More than ten years after the writing of *A Cidade e a Infância*, Luandino's second novel returns to the fragmentation of past collectivity and, more important, to the reinvention of that past. The question that ends the novel—"We, those of Makulusu?"—or more aptly put, leaves the novel open-ended, concerns the survival not only of the "we" but also of the values of that specific past. As Luandino himself has pointed out, "Makulusu has disappeared irrevocably." The question posed by the novel's narrator is whether the we, the collective we that has been marked by the positive values of Makulusu that emerged from within the boundaries of race, class, and origin, will be able to construct a future based on the communal memory of those very values.[61]

This narrative questioning of both the textualized past and imagined future is prefigured in the novel's Kimbundu epigraph that translates into English as: "Because from where we come there isn't anything left to see. What we look for is where we are going." This epigraph, cited as from a "traditional tale," is actually from the Kimbundu maka "Kututunda Ni Kutuia" ("The Past and the Future") included in Héli Chatelain's *Folk Tales of Angola*. In this tale, two men—Kututunda ("Whence-we-come") and Kutuia ("Where-we-go")—request wine from a palm-wine tapper. The tapper refuses Kutuia on the grounds that his name (the future) represents evil. The judge who hears the maka between Kutuia and the tapper decides in favor of the future, and *Nós, os do Makulusu*'s opening epigraph represents the reasoning behind that judgment. Only the future provides an answer to the open ending, whether history will permit the survival of the we of Makulusu.

The novel's interrogative discourse follows the stream of consciousness narration of Mais-Velho, the oldest child of Portuguese peasants who have settled in Angola.[62] The death of his younger brother, Maninho, an officer in the Portuguese army in Angola, serves as the immediate catalyst for the narrative: "Simple, simple, just like that a shot: he was an officer, took a bullet, went to war and poured his life on the ground, it drank the blood."[63] The syntax of the sentence is Kimbundu, most noticeably in the last part, which in standard English would really read "the blood drank." The reference, though, is to the ground soaking in the blood. The subsequent narrative, however, negates the "simple, simple" both of Maninho's death and its recounting. Salvato Trigo notes that the stream-of-consciousness narration is associative rather than chronological and impedes an easy reading of the text.[64] The narrative movement follows relations triggered by the stream of consciousness, and the resulting complexity has led at least one critic to misread the novel at its most literal level.[65]

Nós, os do Makulusu's reinvention of the past is further complicated by the position of the narrator, Mais-Velho. His narration takes place several years after the death of his brother and involves an overlapping of temporalities. For instance, the recounting of Maninho's funeral combines events of the past, present, and future. These events are perceived by Mais-Velho, who at the same time relives the experiences and their emotional impact through their recreation as narrative.

The reinventions of the past move among familial scenes, conversations between the narrator and his friends, and depictions of the idealized and hybrid childhood in the musseque of Makulusu. Events are recalled repeatedly but always with the incorporation of new elements to provide an integral vision of the past. Certain motifs appear throughout the text—"we, those of Makulusu" and "bilinguals that we almost are," for instance—and represent, as Luandino Vieira states, "theorizations" or a type of spontaneous and questioning commentary on the narration itself.[66] These narrative theorizations and reflections lead to the last question — "We, those of Makulusu?" — and to the narrator's final understanding of the destruction of the collectivity.

The narrative reinvention of the we provokes, in this way, a parallel realization of its breakdown. This breakdown is first perceived in the immediate violence of the nationalist struggle but also encompasses the extended history of political and sociocultural conflicts in Angola. The we, therefore, indeed represents the four friends and brothers from Makulusu (Mais-Velho, Maninho, their mulatto half-brother, Paizinho, and their friend, Kibiaka), but it also incorporates a more totalizing vision of Portuguese colonialism. As part of the integral historicizing of the narration, Mais-Velho's introspections, retrospections, and interrogations bring to light the many boundaries installed by five centuries of Portuguese domination.

The stream-of-consciousness narration also accompanies Mais-Velho's wanderings through Luanda. As in Luandino's estórias and A Vida Verdadeira de Domingos Xavier, the reclaiming of Angolan discursive space always involves a parallel reclaiming of the geographical space of Luanda. Here, as the narrator passes through certain streets and sections of the city, the landmarks, shops, restaurants, and so forth trigger related memories of the collective we but always within the totalizing vision of history. Thus one of Mais-Velho's recollections of Maninho's funeral provokes a simultaneous imagining of violent colonial history: "Chains of slaves, chains of the dead, of prisoners, of contract laborers, of the free—a whole history to unearth."[67] Nós, os do Makulusu is of course the partial unearthing of that history and the breaking, so to speak, of the chains that can only be cast off once that history is restored to those who were enslaved, prisoners, contract laborers, and even free people in an imagined Angolan nation.

In this sense, the countering of chronological narrative time must be read as much more than a mere experimentation with acculturated structures. Barbara Harlow's study indicates that resistance narratives experiment with linear temporality as an essential part of the struggle to claim a totalizing history. Part of this challenge is what Harlow terms "a radical rewriting" of the European historiographies that privilege the western calendar of events.[68] In Nós, os do Makulusu, that radical rewriting implies a reclaiming of Angolan history through a reimagining of the conditions of hybridity.

As was the case with Luandino's earlier textualizations of past collectivity in A Cidade e a Infância, the narrative imagining of a hybrid we always reveals a tense, if not violent, coexistence. In the earlier stories, the reinventions of the past were conditioned by the fragmentation precipitated by the white settler influx and the destruction of those conditions that had permitted a racial-cultural proximation. Clearly Nós, os do Makulusu moves beyond fragmentation and displacement. The immediate setting of the novel captures the total rupture of the we, while the introspections expose the contradictions that marked the violent collectivity. In this sense, the positive visions of the creolized childhood world of *A Cidade e a Infância* appear in the 1967 novel as no less a determining force, but they are always countered by the realizations of colonial relations of appropriation and inequality.

As in the earlier narratives of *A Cidade e a Infância*, the breakdown of collectivity follows the movement from childhood to adolescence to adulthood. The fragmentation—textualized in such previous works as "Encontro de Acaso," "A Fronteira de Asfalto," and "A Cidade e a Infância"—intensifies with the boundaries that mark the adult world in the stratified colonial society. In *Nós, os do Makulusu*, the diverse paths of the four childhood friends and brothers demonstrate the rupture of collectivity. Maninho, as Russell Hamilton points out, represents a new colonialist mentality that continues within the sphere of white racial-cultural superiority, even though paradoxically he has "undergone his measure of creolization."[69] Maninho, however, is conscious of the contradictions of colonial domination but points to those very racial-cultural relations of inequality as his justification for fighting against Angolan liberation: "This, Mais-Velho, is what is difficult and what I must do. The grass of Makulusu dried beneath the tar pavement and we grew up. And while we can't understand each other because only one side of us grew, we must kill one another; that is the reason for our lives, the only manner that I can give fraternally to allow him to assume his dignity—kill or be killed, on our feet." [70] Maninho's reasoning indeed recognizes the breakdown of collectivity that he describes as a necessarily unequal coexistence dictated by the nonreciprocal acculturation process. However, he seeks a paradoxical measure of equality through armed confrontation. Mais-Velho and Paizinho follow the course of clandestine organization and political education. Kibiaka, embodying a reasoning that counters that of Maninho, joins the armed nationalists.

The novel's final question voices the realization of fragmentation—the disappearance of Makulusu and all that it represented—and rupture, the destruction of the we. Ultimately, the narrator, like the judge deciding the maka between the future and the wine-tapper, views the destruction of the past as necessary violence, so that a future based on relations of equality might be constructed: "Your relative will become my absolute—solidarity, is it like this?—and it will also calm me, having the certainty that later I will destroy and destroying I will reconstruct and go on like this, with you who is not you, but us, those of Makulusu, constructing not a certainty, but certainties that will help us to be neither cowards nor heroes: only people."[71]

The future remains an uncertainty, an open vision projected from the fragmentation of past collectivity and the rupture of present conflict. The narrator may decide in favor of the uncertain future but does not negate the past, however contradictory and fragmented. As resistance narrative, *Nós, os do Makulusu* proposes a reconstruction of the conflictive past and present through subjective and collective narrative memory. In this sense, Mais-Velho's assertion that "life is not time, but only its memory—we've already forgotten that and want to get to the twenty-first century" tempers the open and present conflict that destroys the past and also threatens to negate its memory.[72] The destruction of Makulusu and the we are irreparable and even necessary; the narrative questions whether that which might survive can be both remembered and reconciled in the imagined future nation.

Neologizing Nation

> We don't use Portuguese because someone gave us authorization,
> or because of a statute, or due to a mandate, or from charity. It is a
> trophy of war.[73]
> José Luandino Vieira

For Luandino Vieira, the process of imagining a nation can only be realized through the invention of a language that is itself hybrid and nonhierarchical. In spite of his claim that Angolan writers have gained the Portuguese language as a spoil of war, the fight for discursive terrain has not meant a simple wholesale appropriation of acculturated literary discourse any more than his elaboration of the estória has implied a facile borrowing of Portuguese narrative forms. If the estória celebrates the reclaiming of narrative terrain, indeed the right to collective narration, then Luandino's language is no less resistant and popular.

Even the earliest of Luandino's narratives attempt to incorporate a hybrid language that is based on popular practices of creolization so that the discourses of the marginal become the voices of imagining nationness and Angolan identities. The use of such a language is part of transculturation as a claiming of imposed structures that are then made Angolan. The language in which these narrative voices speak are themselves acts of resistance that work against assimilation practices of the New State, which would not acknowledge local patterns of creolization, but instead inextricably tied the use of a standard language to social mobility and rights of citizenship. This is a language, then, that counters acculturation and also becomes a means of resistance, both for the characters and for the readers. If Luandino employs a neologized language based on popular practices, then his works are aimed at a future literate Angola and not the metropolitan marketplace.

In this vein, Luandino took a strong stand against including glossaries in his works, even after independence. It was not until the eighth Portuguese edition of *Luuanda* (1981) that he authorized a glossary of Kimbundu terms, creolized expressions, and neologisms. Until that time, the writer stood steadfast in his position that if metropolitan readers were going to understand his works, they would do so on the terms of the texts themselves and would be forced to surrender to the hybrid language. In the 1980 English-language version of *Luuanda*, which did include a glossary, translator Tamara Bender cites Luandino as explaining that "he wrote his estórias for the very people whose language he used, adding that ignorance of musseque speech was the problem of the Portuguese colonizer, not his."[74]

Thus the language of the works themselves is resistant as it holds back the secrets of the imagined linguistic community and builds collectivity from within this hybrid discourse. As we will see, this resistance of language assumes many forms in the narratives as the collective basis of shared identity and linguistic memory. As an invented language based on popular luandense patterns, it above all envisions nationness as the space in which the peripheral registers are valorized as literary discourses.

Paradoxically, the literary model for Luandino Vieira's inventions of language was not Angolan or even African for that matter, but rather Brazilian. During the author's previously mentioned period of rethinking his notions of narrative, his reading of *Sagarana* by Brazilian writer João Guimarães Rosa suggested a new literary direction: "[A]nd that was what João Guimarães Rosa taught me, that writers have the freedom to create a language that is not that of their characters: a homologue of those characters, of that language. That is to say, what I had to learn from the people was those processes by which they constructed their language . . . using the same unconscious or conscious processes which served the people to use the Portuguese language."[75] For Luandino, then, the lesson of rethinking *Sagarana* in terms of his own literary practice was the freedom to invent a language that was based on the popular patterns of accommodation and resistance in Angola.

The practice of neology, employed somewhat tentatively in *Luuanda*, virtually explodes in *Velhas Estórias*, revised during this time of literary rethinking in Tarrafal. The neologisms in this collection can be divided into four main categories: those derived from Kimbundu; those that have their roots in luandense Portuguese; those that are created from standard Portuguese; and those that represent a creolization of Portuguese and Kimbundu. Examples from the first category include such words as *axuetado* from the Kimbundo *ku xueta* (to dry), *banzanco* and *banzativo* from *ku banza* (to think), *xaxateiro* and *xaxata* from *ku xata* (to squeeze), and *mussequial* from *musseque*. Words such as *tristecido* from the Portuguese *entristecido* (saddened) and *venear* from *envenenar* (to poison) represent the luandense tendency to eliminate the first vocalic syllable.

Neologisms derived from standard Portuguese include fusions of two separate words to form a new one with combined semantic value: *Belzebúnico* (*Belzebu* and *único*) (singular); *cautelento* (*cauteloso* and *lento*) (cautious and slow); *pretazul* (*preto* and *azul*) (black and blue); and *vagamundagem* (*vagabundagem* and *mundo*) (vagabondage and world). Finally, words with both Portuguese and Kimbundu roots include *mexebundo* (*mexer* and *bunda*) and *zulado* (a shortened form of *azulado* that also gains semantic value from the Kimbundu *ku zala*—to be without clothes).[76]

In *Velhas Estórias*, more than one hundred neologisms represent more than a relexification of Portuguese literary language. Luandino's use of Kimbundu-derived words and expressions indicates a valorization of the literary capacity of that language as well as a means of incorporating the voices of its then-marginalized speakers. In the same manner, the creolized neologisms revindicate disparaged speech patterns and simultaneously underscore the positive semantic capacities of the creolization process for the textualization of nation. The creation of words and expressions from various language and dialect systems indicates not only the new directions of an emerging Angolan literature but also the polyglot hybrid possibilities of the imagined nation.

In terms of Luandino's narratives, this practice implies a movement away from the earlier, more direct duplication of luandense speech patterns. Various characters in *A Cidade e a Infância*, for instance, employ creolized speech but mostly at the lexical level. In *A Vida Verdadeira de Domingos Xavier*, however, Kimbundu-Portuguese is introduced into the narrative voice at both the lexical and syntactic levels. Creolized words such as *muxaxar, candengue, cambuta, matumba, quifunes, inbambas,* and *xuaxulhar* are used by both characters and narrator.

In addition, several grammatical patterns prevalent in luandense creolized speech are incorporated into the text. For instance, the preposition *em* is used when the object refers to a person: "*Foi encontrar a comphaneira pondo quifunes em miúdo Bastião;*" "*Vou casar na Bebiana;*" "*Os dois amigos despediram no vavô.*" The indirect object *lhe* (to you, to her, to him) is used in grammatical constructions that in standard Portuguese demand a direct object: "*Nunca lhe vi no musseque;*" "*Ninguém lhe conhecia.*" The subjunctive mode is at times suppressed: "*Talvez Domingos tinha sido levado lá;*" "*Se Maria não tinha sua amiga no Sambizanga, como ia fazer então.*" The subject pronoun *você* ("you" informal) appears with the verb ending that corresponds to the *tu* ("you" intimate) form. The following sentence illustrates all of these syntactic constructions of luandense creolized Portuguese: "*Melhor você dizer naquele homem se mano Xico chega, a gente lhe esperar na muralha.*" The use of these speech patterns by both characters and narrator clearly indicates a shared hybrid literary discourse and further emphasizes the novel's collective vision by means of a common language of resistance.

If *Luuanda*, indeed, marks a turn in Luandino's prose in terms of transculturated and hybridized literary form, that turn also signals the transformation of acculturated literary language. *Luuanda* continues the literary valorization of marginalized and popular speech patterns and introduces a tendency toward the creation of new forms. These neologisms all have their roots in words or expressions used in Luanda that are derived from either popular practice or Kimbundu. Neologisms of Kimbundu origin include *cafucambolar* from *kafukambolo* (*cambalhota*), *cocair* from *ku kaia* (*espreitar*) (to observe) and *uatobar* from *ku toba* (*fazer pouco*) (to make fun of). *Capiangista* (thief) comes from the luandense Portuguese use of *capiango* (theft), whereas *cavalmarinho* is based on the popular pronunciation of *cavalo marinho*.

Although no glossary was provided until 1981, interlingual translations at times are provided in the narration itself, as in the following examples in which the underlined sections represent the equivalent expressions in Portuguese:

> *Ri os dentes brancos dela, parece são conchas, xuculula-lhe, mas não é raiva nem desprezo, tem uma escondida satisfação nesse <u>revirar dos olhos</u>.*

> *Nga Tita chegou mais perto para contar a menina nascera cassanda, isso mesmo vavó, nasceu <u>branca, branca</u>, parecia era ainda filha de ngueta.*

> Logo-logo veio um *<u>guisado de feijão</u>, um cheiroso quitande amarelo*.[77]

For the most part, however, translations are not provided so that although *Luuanda*'s estórias refrain from the almost didactic political message of *A Vida Verdadeira de Domingos Xavier* and *Vidas Novas*, political solidarity is expressed through a collective language. Moreover, this is evident within the estórias themselves as the language of resistance establishes the strength of the musseque community. In "Estória da Galinha e do Ovo," for instance, the maka between the two women is not resolved by the outside Portuguese or assimilado judges who attempt to obtain the egg for themselves through discourses of power. Rather the resolution relies on shared codes of resistance in which even the cackle of the hen partakes. José Ornelas notes that truth in this case resides in the art of the colonized who refuse to assimilate the colonial discourse and whose actions subvert monolingualism.[78] A comparison also might be made to Luandino's earlier story, "O Fato Completo de Lucas Matesso" from *Vidas Novas*, in which the imprisoned title character drives his Portuguese jailers and torturers crazy when he asks his wife to bring him a *fato completo*, which in standard continental Portuguese is a man's suit. The authorities search through Matesso's clothing to find a hidden weapon or note, but their search is in vain because they don't realize that in luandense Portuguese a fato completo is the name of a popular fish dish. The prisoner, though beaten from the continued interrogations, laughs at the victory of resistance on the part of a community that has subverted and transformed colonial discourse.

Velhas Estórias, revised during Luandino's literary rethinking in Tarrafal, demonstrates the new linguistic direction through a creative practice based on the recreation of popular patterns of linguistic resistance. It is no coincidence, therefore, that the first estória, "Muadié Gil, o Sobral e o Barril" (Boss Gil, Sobral and the barrel), concerning the dispute over a barrel of wine normally given workers after completion of a construction project, follows the parallel linguistic confrontation between Sobral—the self-appointed voice of the workers—and the Portuguese boss, Gil. The animosity that already exists between the two men because of Gil's attentions to Sobral's wife surfaces in their linguistic dual: "Boss Mr. Gil Afonso! Oh, boss, you old rooster, if you want to fight, take off your spurs."[79] When Gil attempts to respond in his Kimbundu *estragado de branco* (his corrupted white-man's Kimbundu), Sobral retorts: "Hey, boss. Prohibited in the decree! Kimbundu is not official! A white man can't speak Kimbundu."[80] Sobral is the one who controls because of his Kimbundu domain.

The confrontation between the two intensifies when Gil sees one of the workers preparing coffee on the job, and Sobral diverts his attention by means of a linguistic frontal attack:

—*Savá, mestre?*
—*Sou um prolixo, falo línguas maudiê . . . Isto aqui é frenxe!*
—*Prolixo! Pròlixo, é que te mando outra vez.*[81]

Sobral's use of French ("*savá*" for "*ça va*") and English ("*frenxe*" for "French") and his assertion that he is *prolixo* is countered by Gil's play on the word *prolixo* as *pròlixo* ("*para o lixo*"—in the trash).

The linguistic dual takes on overt political dimensions as Gil demands that his workers greet the colonial governor with signs that read "*Os operários da Gilafo/com firmeza na defeza/da Angola portugueza"* (The workers of Gilafo/with strength in the defense/of a Portuguese Angola). The workers look on as the verbal war continues between Sobral and Gil—*"maca de sungarigengo e cangundo fica de fora o monabundo"* (blacks stay out of the maka between mulattos and whites). When Gil explains his rising costs in technical terms, Sobral concedes the advantage: "Sobral could well see that the boss was winning; those words that they didn't know were scoring points."[82]

Although the workers eventually receive the wine, the linguistic dual remains unresolved. Sobral's final song—in Kimbundu, of course—places the confrontation in the larger political-linguistic context. The song also underscores the link between political and cultural independence as it recognizes the Portuguese language as a stratifying and repressive element of colonialism and even neocolonialism: "Portuguese Government!/Portuguese Government! Portuguese Government with good lines/If you don't eat us in the war/ You'll want to eat us in conversations."[83]

A similar linguistic confrontation forms one of the central themes of *Macundumba*'s "Cangundos, Verdianos, Santomistas, Nossa Gente." In this estória, the repeated interpolations of the narrator concern the languages of the musseque as well as the actual narration itself.[84]

The estória textualizes the linguistic hybridity of the musseque as an intersection of Joaquim Ferreira's *"pretoguês,"* Robertom's Cape Verdean creole, Alceu and Marília's pretentious upper-class speech, as well as Kimbundu, legal Portuguese, and creolized musseque discourse. Pretoguês was a pejorative colonial term used to describe the Portuguese spoken by Africans and comes from a combination of *preto* (black) and *português*. Luandino uses the term here somewhat ironically, of course, to describe the assimilation of the Portuguese Joaquim Ferreira into the musseque.

The narrative voice also participates in the confusion of the languages in the estória that adds to the mystery surrounding the counterfeit lottery ticket. If on the one hand the author of the creolized song that opens the text is criticized humorously as an illiterate poet for writing *santomista* instead of the standard santomense (someone from São Tomé), the narrator also freely uses *santomista* throughout the estória. At one point, the narrator uses the verb *fitucar* and interrupts the estória to comment on both meaning and usage: "It was there that sister Marília *fitucou*—as the loyal Ximinha would say, vendor with confidence in the state of the soul at the garden door. Fitucou, that's what it is, there is no foreign word for the feeling of the musseque: hot and wordy anger, with the soul on the outside, all the truths spoken with nothing left out—more friendship than anger, less hate than heat, how is it in the vernacular? Dona Marília, therefore, fitucou."[85] The verb must remain, for there is no outside linguistic means of expressing the musseque. The multiple sociolinguistic registers of Luanda— *"cidade de muitas e mussecadas gentes"* (city of many and musseque-ed peoples) enter into the narrative because, as the title of the estória indicates, they all belong to "nossa gente" (our people).

Sobral, from *Velhas Estórias*, has a counterpart in João Vêncio, also a self-proclaimed "prolixo," whose first-person narration is a hybrid interweaving of languages and linguistic registers. Vêncio self-identifies as an *ambaquista*, and indeed his radical discourse is signaled by the estória's subtitle— *uma tentativa de ambaquismo literário a partir do calão, gíria e termos chulos* (an attempt at literary *ambaquismo* using jargon, slang, and the terms of pimps). As an attempt at literary ambaquismo, the text draws upon the historical role of the Ambacas, whose propensity for argumentation and use of the Portuguese language accounts for their significant part in the colonial administrative and judicial systems. The Ambacas not only served as scribes and notaries for the often illiterate Portuguese colonizers, but they also functioned as provisional lawyers. Here "ambaquista" not only designates origin but also draws its meaning as a popular pejorative expression from those same rhetorical capabilities. Alfredo Margarido suggests, though, that the ambaquistas subverted their own privileged positions to identify with the community, as many became types of public writers.[86] The estória's literary transculturation, suggested by "literary ambaquismo," is informed also by marginalized discourses that are incorporated into the oftentimes rhetorical narration.

João Vêncio continually claims that words lie as they transform reality and truth, although this questioning realization does not stop him from participating in an orchestration of those same lying words: "You're astonished by my vocabulary, my patois? . . . Anyway, my father it was that got me hooked: he gave me the dictionary opened and shut, I learned it by heart. Then, too, my shantytown, with its thousand colors of people, its thousand voices—I'm partial to Verdean lingo, all those neat words! And the rivers of my days, my ways: I was also a tour guide, you know, showing the sailors, the sights, clubs, hussies and sluts. I learned some English. Gee! the clean dirty smell of this sweet old she-rat . . . How much? Twenty dollars? Vêncio, tell this old crab I would rather fuck myself. . . . Ay-ay! My bad ways, parlances!"[87]

João Vêncio's estória is not only his life's multiple stories but also the various discourses that he has absorbed along the way. An accumulation of the codes of standard and popular Portuguese, creolized musseque speech, Cape Verdean creole, English, French, seminary Latin, and biblical discourse all combine to form João Vêncio's hybrid lexicon, or as he puts it, his *"patua"* (patois). It is Vêncio who controls his patois, however, as he mocks at the astonishment of the literate muadiê. Clearly João Vêncio's language is that of colonized hybrid identity and is meant to evoke the multiplicity of his life stories as well as the multiple levels of resistance.

It is language as well that memorializes the tense collective childhood world of *Nós, os do Makulusu*. One of the motifs that runs through the novel, "bilinguals that we are, almost," reveals the frontiers of coexistence as the imagined collective bilingualism is modified by a colonial style "almost."[88] The narrator attempts to remember and indeed reconstruct through language that collective world of Makulusu as he wanders through Luanda, and his memory is triggered by various words and phrases. For instance, Mais-Velho's path through Luanda, specifically through the Bairro dos Coqueiros, leads him to the Rua das Flores (Street of Flowers), which sets off the memory of buying flowers for Maninho's funeral from Dona Marijosé.

Moreover, Mais-Velho fully realizes his own part in the betrayal of the collective we through the recurring recollections of the four friends and brothers trapped in the Makokaloji cave. He desperately attempts to recall the full Kimbundu phrase—he almost has it, almost—that united the four and released them, in his memory, from the cave: "*Ukamba, uakamba kikunda!*" (In friendship there is no betrayal.) It is only at the novel's end that he finds the missing word that signifies his own betrayal.

Undoubtedly, this forgetting of the Kimbundu phrase that marked the unity of the *nós* (we) underscores the conflictive colonial relations of collectivity. The lost Kimbundu phrase further resonates against Maninho's own justification for the war and the suppression, or forgetting, of African and creolized values. Mais-Velho remembers the missing word too late, for he has already betrayed Paizinho by arranging a meeting to tell him the news of their brother's death: "I'm going to see Paizinho, I'm going to meet him, against all the rules of security, against the order that he gave me. . . . And I am betraying, and that is betraying him."[89] Mais-Velho also assumes the guilt for the deaths of the others. He had given Kibiaka a gun when his friend had left Luanda to join the MPLA. He later convinces himself that Kibiaka is the guerrilla who killed Maninho and is killed, in turn, by Portuguese soldiers. The remembrance of that missing word that might reunite the we—even in narrative memory—simultaneously triggers Mais-Velho's realization of his own contradictory position and the irreparable destruction of the collective we: "We have to do what we have to do even if Maninho is laughing—and he isn't laughing now, he's only dead—and curses us since these are society's games, there isn't any other path: . . . to fight so that your reason is not reason and you live and Kibiaka lives and all the dead can live and all the living can die without being heroes. And suddenly, I now remember the third word: *kikunda*, betrayal, that's it and I say:—Ukamba uakamba kikunda!—we leave the depths of death in Makokaloji. And this is now worthless. There is Paizinho under arrest, over there, some one hundred meters from me."[90]

The memory of the childhood game in which the we pronounced the magic words and were released from the Makokaloji cave of death comes too late for Mais-Velho. All alone now, he says the words, but they have lost their magical powers of collective freedom that they had within the violent hierarchies and boundaries of colonial Luanda. Mais-Velho's ultimate narrative question amid the rupture of the we is whether those words might once again recapture the magical and imagined collectivity within the future possibilities of nationness.

This narrative memorialization through language attains its most complex form in No Antigamente, na Vida (In the long ago, in life). The three estórias in this 1974 collection move beyond imagined communal memory to a type of mythicizing of the past. The specific past once again is that of tense childhood collectivity in a colonized and creolized Luanda. In "Lá em Tetembuatubia" (There in Tetembuatubia), language is the key to both the mysterious imagined voyage of the children as well as its textualization. Similar to Mais-Velho's realization that even the remembrances of collectivity might not survive the present rupture of armed conflict, the narrator of "Lá, em Tetembuatubia" also realizes that the return to the past is always inadequate. Here the narrator is the childhood chronicler of the imagined voyages of the musseque children, and even though he obeys their leader's command—"O que ves, escreve-o num livro" (What you see, write it in a book)—he understands the futility of remembering: "Today, Tetembuatubia is not even a simple name on the wall of time. . . . But there was life in its entirety, the place where we found impossible miracles, in a far away long ago."[91]

"The wall of time" (a parede do tempo) is an image that Luandino borrowed and modified from Brazilian poet Carlos Drummond de Andrade's "Confidência do Itabirano." He uses the image in the closing of "Cangundos, Verdianos, Santomistas, Nossa Gente," as the Cape Verdean Robertom dreams of returning home: "On the wall of time, Luanda, that will only be a murmured sound of waters against the hard rocks over there on his island, in the returns."[92]

The images of the wall of time and the many returns for those who are exiled both within and away from their homelands serve as encapsulating metaphors for Luandino's textualizations of nation. His counternarratives to acculturated discourse write against Western notions of chronological time that would colonize Angolan narrative itself in a sequential and false ordering of communal memory and orality that would further separate the past from the future. Luandino Vieira's resistance texts propose transculturated forms and languages to narrate the estórias of Angolan nationness, its imagined pasts, and its possible futures.

The narrator of "Cangundos, Verdianos, Santomistas, Nossa Gente" may project a time-bound image of Luanda but counters this very image with another: "City of truth that no longer exists, never more, it will only be found again one day in a faraway land. And there, it will seem like nothing we've seen or lived—it is the other thing, the veiled light living in the heart, a dewy and serene mist within those who are in exile."[93]

The wall of time, that seemingly eternal colonial boundary that enforces dominant history through European time, remains as a marker of the colonial past in the narratives but is always countered by the collective image of that other Luuanda that stays secreted away in the heart to be narrated as visions of imagined nation. The liberating reclaiming of an integral Angolan past is the telling and retelling of multiple estórias within Luandino Vieira's narratives. By drawing formally from oral traditional structures and by inventing a language that reinvents the polyglot possibilities of Luanda's hybrid community, Luandino imagines an Angolan nation that is at its heart a collective retaking of community and homeland.

Chapter 3

Mimicry in the Contact Zone

Menacing the Colonizers

Uanhenga Xitu was born in 1924 in the Calomboloca village in the Luandan region of Icolo e Bengo. Baptized as Agostinho Mendes de Carvalho, Xitu uses his Kimbundu birth name, which he has always emphasized is not a pen name. Xitu was one of the original organizers of the MPLA and was imprisoned between 1959 and 1970 in Luanda and Tarrafal. Since Angolan independence, Xitu has served as a member of the Central Committee of the MPLA, as minister of health, and as ambassador to the former East Germany. The author began writing in Tarrafal, and his works were published after 1974.

For Luandino Vieira, the narration of nation is a transculturated practice that reclaims discursive terrain through the invention of hybrid Angolan literary forms and languages. For Uanhenga Xitu, his contemporary and one-time fellow prisoner in the political camp in Tarrafal, narrating the Angolan nation is no less an imagining of hybrid identities but is carried out under subversive strategies of mimicry and farce. Homi Bhabha has suggested the role that mimicry plays in the subversion of colonial discourse by the discriminated subject: "The menace of mimicry is its double vision which in disclosing the ambivalence of colonial discourse also disrupts its authority."[1] Mimicry is menacing precisely because the colonized subject seems to be gazing adoringly at the metropolis, while there is a second gaze behind the adoration that is mocking and carries the threat of disruption.

In Uanhenga Xitu's narratives, this second gaze, masked within the colonial visions of the other, is the one that counts. Xitu mocks the discourses of the Portuguese civilizing mission with a counterstance that seemingly defies hybrid Angolan identity. Behind that public stance, however, is the counterglance that perceives what are not separate, but ambivalent, spaces of hybridity.

Unlike Luandino, whose urban-based narratives memorialize the conditions of tense collectivity, Uanhanga Xitu's ambivalent spaces are those of the rural peripheries outside of Luanda that are imagined as transitional sites. One might expect these peripheral regions to have more clear-cut oppositions than those of Luandino's imagined Luanda. Indeed, Xitu's own public stance as a cultural nationalist would posit a simple, bifurcated struggle between traditional African societies and Portuguese colonizers—the oppressed and the oppressors. In fact the imagined communities that Xitu narrates are far more complex spaces than his public stance suggests.

In a 1983 interview, Uanhenga Xitu affirmed his commitment to the literary recuperation of traditional sectors and also cited the necessity to preserve the knowledge of their cultural practices: "The city is wasted and there are other sad things to be said about city life. I will continue to talk about the forest, forest things, because many of our comrades don't know what is going on there and what exists there. I will continue to speak about things such as bride-price. Not as it's done today, which isn't anything. . . . We have to face our cultural reality. Our literature is oral and is fundamentally guarded by old people and they are dying. With them also dies the great African (Angolan) cultural richness."[2]

Here Xitu's public stance indicates the various narrative tensions that mark his works. The immediate conflict that Xitu himself cites between the urban and rural sectors denotes one of the central and recurring themes of his prose fiction. The overt dichotomy, however, also signals deeper tensions and ambiguities of cultural hybridity. In this interview Xitu describes the city as a type of cultural wasteland, whereas the true cultural reality of Angola—a literature that is oral—is practiced in the rural zones. Of course the danger here is that this too is dying out with the death of an older generation and the veiled threat of modern practices.

Finally, Xitu's 1983 interview suggests a confrontation of cultural values from a postcolonial perspective. The use of "our comrades" evokes the revolutionary socialist political formation that defined important sectors of the nationalist liberation struggle. Here, part of the revolutionary idiom is juxtaposed to the traditional *alambamento* (bride-price) that is incompatible with revolutionary socialist goals. Moreover, Xitu promises only to speak of the true alambamento of the past and not the contemporary, diluted practice.

Xitu's narratives, however, are set within colonial Angola and on the surface envision the rural sectors as areas of conflict between traditional and colonial practices. In this sense, Xitu's fiction bears similarities to that of an earlier Angolan writer, António Assis Júnior. Both authors assume cultural-nationalist positions but narrate the tense cultural ambiguities of colonial Angola. Whereas Assis Júnior's *O Segredo da Morta* belies his cultural-purist stance, the ambivalences of Xitu's fiction are actually cultivated in narratives that both mimic and subvert colonial discourse.

Beneath the surface dichotomies of Xitu's imaginings of rural colonial Angola are the conflictive spaces of hybrid transculturated practices and identities. Mary Louise Pratt refers to these spaces of colonial encounters as "contact zones" and explains that a contact perspective "treats the relations among colonizers and colonized . . . not in terms of separateness or apartheid, but in terms of copresence, interaction, interlocking understanding and practices, often within radically asymmetrical relations of power."[3] Pratt's perspective here is an actual decentering of community identity (and indeed, one could argue, national identity) in favor of examining social and historical interactions across differences and hierarchies.[4] Uanhenga Xitu textualizes nationness in these spaces of conflictive contact both among colonial subjects and within imagined individuals. His appropriation of metropolitan modes of representation assumes a mocking stance as often-extravagant elaborations of acculturated discourse. Mimicry's double vision is ambiguous, however, as are the subject representations of hybrid identities in Uanhenga Xitu's narrations of nation.

The Pitfalls of Hybridity

Uanhenga Xitu began writing in prison while serving a ten-year sentence for political activities against the Portuguese New State. He was in the Tarrafal prison camp from 1962 to 1970 in the company of other imprisoned militant writers, including António Jacinto, Luandino Vieira, and Helder Neto. The narratives written in prison — "Mestre" Tamoda, "Bola com Feitiço," *Vozes na Sanzala, Maka na Sanzala,* and *Manana* — were published only after the fall of the Portuguese fascist regime in 1974. Xitu recalls that his work did not escape the notice of prison authorities: "I remember that 'Mestre' Tamoda was taken and burned two times by authorities in the Casa da Reclusão of Angola prison and in Tarrafal."[5] During my personal interview with the author on July 23, 1985, he showed me originals of some of the prison narratives. Some were written on brown wrapping paper, and Xitu recounted how he oftentimes buried these writings in the ground to hide them from prison authorities. "Mestre" Tamoda was first edited in Lobito in June 1974 in the Cadernos Capricórnio series but was reissued in 1977 by Edições 70 (Lisbon) in an edition that also included "Bola com Feitiço" and *Vozes na Sanzala*. Xitu's first published fiction is also that for which the writer is best known. The novella focuses on the linguistic and cultural confrontations that arise when Tamoda, the Kimbundu nickname of Domingos João Adão, returns to his native *sanzala* (rural village) after spending his adolescent years in Luanda. The conflicts produced by the opposing cultures of the traditional sanzala and the colonial city provide the basis of Xitu's narrative of sociocultural and linguistic confrontations and contradictions.

These contradictions are manifested most clearly in Tamoda, who after his formation and experiences in Luanda returns to his birthplace to find a wife and settle down. He descends upon the village as a "new intellectual" replete with his own personal library that includes many old novels, a worm-eaten dictionary plus some additional dictionary pages, a book on how to write love letters, and some volumes of law. Tamoda had learned to read and write in Luanda and at his last job took advantage of his employer's frequent absences to advance his education. His knowledge is selective, though, and based on the appropriation and manipulation of those words that appeal to his aesthetic sense.

Tamoda's discriminating linguistic practice establishes an immediate conflict with the Kimbundu-speaking villagers: "The new intellectual, in the middle of a village in which almost all of its inhabitants spoke Kimbundu and only in special cases used Portuguese, thought himself the highest point of the language of Camões."[6] The conflict is further exacerbated by Tamoda's inventive but malapropos use of a Portuguese linguistic register that defies comprehension. He is dubbed *"mestre"* (literally meaning "master" but here taking on the meaning of "teacher" as well) due to his linguistic daring, and he cultivates disciples among the village youth, who repeat Tamoda's *putos caros* (fine words). This last expression means a Portuguese word and is derived from *Putu*, the Kimbundu name for Portugal.

Soon after, Tamoda is ordered to appear at the colonial administrative post. The reasons listed in the summons underscore the linguistic and cultural conflicts provoked by his return to the village: "He had been denounced as a sluggard and without documents. Also the fact that he nicknamed the African policemen hangmen or *fintilhos*, and the *regedores*, *panacas* or *picaios*, created bad feelings toward him among the authorities. Independent of that, the hairdos that had been introduced among young people, in order to have hair like his, had caused burns on their heads."[7]

At the administrative post, Tamoda antagonizes the *mais-velhos*, or elders, because of his exaggerated European mannerisms and lack of respect. The *cipaios* (African police) also take notice of Tamoda, and one of them blames the influence of the city for the disrespect of the younger generation. Tamoda's interview with the colonial administrator follows a similar course, as the latter is less than impressed with Tamoda's incomprehensible Portuguese. Moreover, his documents are not in order, and the official not only fines Tamoda but also bans him from spreading city vices in the village. One of the cipaios sums up the experience by noting that all of Tamoda's Portuguese is worthless if he doesn't have the proper documents.

On one level, *"Mestre" Tamoda* provides a humorous account of the cultural conflicts that arise from Tamoda's encounters within various social strata of the rural zone. Undoubtedly a space of contentious practices, the village contact zone is not the traditional and pure haven that a simplistic dichotomy might project. Within the slippages of the narrative discourse, we learn that Portuguese is indeed spoken on special occasions in the village—and here we can only assume that they are occasions of contact with the colonizers—and that the village school instructs in Portuguese as well. Tamoda wreaks havoc in the sanzala, not because he puts on the airs of an assimilado but because his mimicry takes assimilation to an excess. If, as Bhabha claims, the desire of colonial mimicry is "for a reformed recognizable Other, as a subject of difference that is almost the same," Tamoda becomes a menace to colonial society because his perceived "Other" is neither reformed nor recognizable.[8] In other words, he has moved outside of the prescribed acculturated boundaries of the colonized Other and, instead, intervened in colonial discourse by means of self-representation.

That this self-representation is the excess of mimicry and ultimately farcical serves to disrupt the colonial order and mocks the farce of the Portuguese civilizing mission itself. Tamoda presents himself culturally—but certainly not legally, as he doesn't even have the proper documents—as an assimilado, and he has the books to prove it. These books—novels of Portuguese valor, outdated dictionaries, manuals on how to write love letters and other assorted correspondence, compendiums of laws and regulations—prescribe the forms of acculturation, the mocking assumption of course being the actual vacuous nature of the civilizing mission. If Tamoda represents himself as partaking in the language of Camões, the reminder here is of a colonizing of epic proportions with Tamoda overplaying the role of the colonized village savant.

Critics of *"Mestre" Tamoda* have tended to read the narrative in terms of the title character's marginalized position—he is alienated from both the traditional society and scorned by the colonial apparatus. These same critics, however, claim that Tamoda practices cultural resistance because he appropriates and utilizes the language of colonization as a means of contestation.[9]

What is being overlooked, is that "*Mestre*" *Tamoda* is a farce, not pure nor simple, but a farce nonetheless of the Portuguese civilizing mission. The readings of Tamoda as a figure of cultural resistance are utopic in that they seek a (proto)revolutionary behind every mask of mimicry. The confusion here, of course, ultimately lies between Xitu's narrative as resistance and its depiction of Tamoda as an ambivalent hybrid figure. As writer Manuel Rui notes, Tamoda remains a ridiculous figure precisely because he lacks the political consciousness to conquer his alienation and to transform those very instruments of colonization into arms against colonial domination.[10] The narrative's three-line resolution—Tamoda goes back to the sanzala and dies many years later without his shirt, shoes, or helmet—is a structural one only and remains undeveloped as well as unexplained.

As a narrative of mimicry, "*Mestre*" *Tamoda* mocks colonial discourse through the confrontation of different languages of representation within the stratified colonial space of contact. Salvato Trigo prefers to describe this confrontation as an interpenetration of languages and claims that the resulting linguistic polyphony present in all of Xitu's narratives actually represents textual *griotismo* in written narratives being transformed by techniques of orature.[11] Undoubtedly, Trigo's position finds support in Uanhenga Xitu's own public stance, and while works such as *Vozes na Sanzala* and *Maka na Sanzala* may be read in part as narrational writing of oral storytelling practices, Trigo's analysis ignores the ambivalent basis of Xitu's fiction. This is further seen in his assessment of Xitu's narrative as marked by discursive mestiçagem.[12] Here, as often occurs, mestiçagem assumes an unproblematic synthesis that belies the confrontations and contradictions of Xitu's narratives.

In contrast, Russell Hamilton identifies five linguistic registers present in Xitu's narrative fiction. These registers are: the standard Portuguese narration that is tempered by Angolan terms; the use of Kimbundu in both analytical and colloquial contexts; technical Portuguese used in footnotes and glossaries to explain African cultural practices; the authoritarian Portuguese of colonists and administrators; and the Portuguese spoken by colonized African subjects.[13] As will be developed in the discussion of Uanhenga Xitu's other works, the author's manipulation of the different languages of the contact zone serves primarily as the basis for counternarratives that mimic and subvert colonial discourse. The languages and linguistic registers that inform Xitu's narrative discourse function as socio-ideological indicators of the different contact groups within the textualizations of colonial Angola. Xitu's narrative orchestration of languages, however, defies Salvato Trigo's assessment of linguistic polyphony, for the resulting multileveled discourse is anything but harmonious and in fact might be better deemed cacophonous. Moreover, Xitu's contact zones often seem more like combat zones in which the confrontations of the antagonistic groups emerge as a sociolinguistic struggle.

In *"Mestre" Tamoda*, the title character moves from one zone of contact (Luanda) to another (the sanzala) bringing with him what he believes to be a prestigious linguistic register and the promise of a relatively privileged social position within the realm of colonial cultural assimilation. As mimicry, the mestre's selective and incomprehensible Portuguese serves no such function either in the sanzala or in the administrative post. He is comically trapped between the two cultures as a pastiche, of sorts, of colonial cultural hybridity. Tamoda's self-representation is all the more menacing, though, because in its extravagant excess it threatens to expose the facade of Portuguese acculturation.

Ten years after the first edition of *"Mestre" Tamoda*, the master returned in a second work, *Os Discursos do "Mestre" Tamoda* (The discourses of "Master" Tamoda). Uanhenga Xitu informed me that this work originally had been written in prison and would have been included in the first "Mestre" Tamoda narrative had it not been seized by prison authorities.[14] The six discourses, although published together as chapters in book-length form, are actually autonomous vignettes that focus on colonial societies in both the sanzala and Luanda. The chapters are unified by Tamoda's discourses, but unlike *"Mestre" Tamoda*, the title character does not assume a central role. Rather, he appears incidental to several of the episodes and in some cases seems to be almost a pretext for the particular narrative.

This is not to say that there is a radical thematic shift between the two "Mestre" Tamoda texts. The conflicts of the first narrative are central to Xitu's later imagining of the contact zones; one of the vignettes is set among the colonial bourgeoisie of Luanda. The most significant shift is that of the narrative perspective. The narrator of *Os Discursos do "Mestre" Tamoda* assumes an interpolative role, and not unlike the narrators of Xitu's other works of fiction, as will be discussed shortly, the narrator interrupts the narrative movement to insert other incidents, directly address the readers, or offer metatextual remarks on the various linguistic registers. The most essential shift, however, lies in the 1984 narrator's role as a type of social commentator who narrates from an informed historical perspective, whether in terms of conveying the ethnological background of certain traditional practices or of commenting on the unequal social relations of the 1930s colonial period.

For example, in the episode concerning Tamoda's widowed *prima co-irmã* (cousin co-sister) and the rites of remarriage, the narrator begins with a commentary on the contemporary perversion of traditional customs through contact with European civilization and church influences: "And thus today we see civilized blacks and mulattoes getting married to 'cousin co-sisters' and with nieces, before the shock of the old women who consider this *kisunji* (abomination, incest) or a crime meriting death for whoever committed it in the time of their ancestors."[15] The narrator here assumes not only a position of cultural revindication but also one of cultural purism as he comments on the contradictory present-day practices before embarking on his narration of the past.

This purist stance clashes with the imagined sociocultural relations of 1930s luandense society, as depicted in the final chapter concerning the staged marriage between Marajá and Arlete. Contradictions abound in the creolized society as members of the Portuguese colonial bourgeoisie, who outwardly maintain European practices for the sake of social appearances, commonly consult *quimbandas* (shamans). Here the acculturation process is seen as somewhat two-way as Dona Josefa, the African housemaid, is described as *muito portuguesona* (extremely Portuguese), and Arlete's mother seeks the aid of a quimbanda to put an end to the supposed romance between Marajá and her daughter. The reciprocal acculturation is anything but equal, given the social, racial, and economic stratifications of the colonial luandense contact zone.

The surface opposition of cultural practices within the urban and rural areas also serves as the point of departure in Uanhenga Xitu's short narrative, "Bola com Feitiço" (Ball with sorcery). The immediate confrontation here, as the title indicates, centers around a soccer game between the teams from neighboring sanzalas. The European soccer acquired by the players in the cities encounters the village practice of *feitiço* (sorcery), and each team employs a quimbanda to perform the traditional rites deemed necessary to secure a victory. The confrontation between the two teams also unmasks the deeper conflict between those characters who abide by the local religious practices and others who have been educated in Protestant missions.

The intrigue of "Bola com Feitiço" develops around the rivalry between the two soccer clubs and their respective quimbandas as well as the confrontation of religious practices. Indeed, the actual soccer match is obscured by ritualistic preparations and after only twenty minutes ends in an open brawl among players and fans. The two quimbandas attribute the fight not to the immediate disagreement over a play but to the underlying confrontation of cultural practices: "These guys from the Missions, when they become involved with *coisas da terra* they always provoke disturbances."[16] "Coisas da terra" literally means "things of the land" and refers to the local and not imposed practices.

The cultural conflict is underscored by a narrative voice that continually interrupts the story in order to explain the underlying meanings of certain actions. When Kahima, the manager of the Calomboloca club, meets with the quimbanda in order to arrange the necessary rituals, the narrator stops to explain that Kahima does not take notes because pencils and sorcery don't mix. According to the narrator, the distrust that quimbandas hold for literate people is so great that they will stop in mid-consultation if the petitioner brings out a pencil or pen to take notes.[17]

The narration is more ambiguous than explanatory, for if on the one hand the narrator describes European practices as being alienated and in opposition to sanzala life, on the other hand the local rituals also are narrated with a certain disbelief. When one of the quimbandas questions a pig as to the outcome of the match, the narrator claims that the pig's grunt is purely coincidental and does not indicate a response. The narrator appears thoroughly versed in local practices, though, and in this sense, the comic recounting of rituals is countered by narrative interpolations that freely combine a relatively standard Portuguese with Kimbundu terminology of sorcery. Although the narrator interrupts to explain the underlying conflicts, the Kimbundu terms are not explained in the narration itself but rather in elaborate footnotes to the story. Footnotes of that type had also appeared in "*Mestre*" *Tamoda* but served primarily as interlingual translations of Kimbundu words and phrases.

In "Bola com Feitiço" the notes are not limited to translations but also provide technical explanations of popular sanzala practices. The use of these interlingual and intercultural notes raises the question of the text's intended audience. Russell Hamilton compares Xitu's use of translations and glossaries to Luandino Vieira's long-term refusal to include either. Hamilton concludes that Xitu's practice assures immediate communication to a wider readership.[18] Undoubtedly the inclusion of notes and translations permits a more immediate textual comprehension not only by non-Angolan readers of Portuguese but also by those Portuguese-speaking Angolans who might not know the local practices and/or languages in question. Xitu's own public stance, which describes his intent to use his writing as a means of traditional cultural preservation, supports the notion that the elaborate notes are meant to facilitate communication.

The explanatory and often didactic tendency of the notes and glossaries is counterposed by the disclosure that at times the more or less standard Portuguese narrative represents an attempt to convey a colloquial Kimbundu expression. In "Bola com Feitiço," when Kahima says "*Aquilo que se recomendar não se discute*" (One doesn't dispute that which is recommended), an accompanying footnote provides the equivalent Kimbundu dictum.[19] The note points to an underlying Kimbundu discourse as well as to the narrative play on linguistic and cultural contacts. Beginning with "Bola com Feitiço," Xitu's narratives expose the mimicry of colonial discourse in the transculturated narratives themselves. Thus the surface function of the narratives as types of cultural go-betweens is always countered, if not undermined, by commentaries on the pitfalls of transculturated discourse.

In *"Mestre" Tamoda,* the mimicry of colonial discourse took the form of excess to mocking extremes in the transculturated narrative. Xitu's subsequent narrations spread the mimicry around, so to speak, so that not only are hybrid individuals up for comic and often tragic grabs, but the hybrid narratives themselves mock their own strains of dominant discourse and thus undermine their own position as "literature." The exaggerated and overtechnical footnotes of "Bola com Feitiço," as well as the narrative commentaries, indicate both the surface subverting put-on of colonial discourse and the deeper questioning of hybrid discourse itself.

This questioning first appears explicitly in *Maka na Sanzala* (Dispute in the sanzala), subtitled "Mafuta." In Uanhenga Xitu's introduction to the text, he explains that his literary practice is based on oral storytelling techniques: "When I remember to stamp a story or short story onto paper, the feeling that surrounds me is that I have to convince myself that I am in front of listeners who are enthusiastically waiting for the moment to listen and to judge me."[20] This concern with re-creating the immediate reception of oral narration is followed by a positioning of the storyteller about to begin the tale: "Therefore, I arrange a comfortable position to better narrate the story, without paying heed to the fact that in the middle of my people, there are some listeners who might influence me, not allowing me to continue the narration."[21]

Although Xitu has just explained that his written narration attempts to re-create the conditions of orature that assume an immediate judgmental reception, at the same time this narrative positioning precludes those very conditions. In this sense, the "comfortable position" can refer to the narrator of written stories who does not have to contend with immediate reception. This somewhat contradictory positioning is further enforced by Xitu's use of the verb *falar* (to speak): "And, now, I will speak to you in a more humble language, that is mine, lacking in adjectives, vocabulary, pompous words and phrases, and without the rigor of punctuation, because I replace all of this with my own gestures and parts."[22] Moreover, the accompanying gesticulations, which Xitu claims will compensate for the poverty of his language, are associated with orature and conflict with the author's own assessment of *Maka na Sanzala* as a written "Kimbundu exercise."

This tension between written and oral narrative sharpens as Xitu explains to his *leitores* (readers) certain salient features of spoken Kimbundu of the Icolo e Bengo region. He ends the introduction by again referring to the written narrative and cites the "approximate translation into Portuguese" that accompanies Kimbundu words and expressions. This introductory positioning—the self-presentation of the author, so to speak—situates itself within a negotiated and imagined terrain between orature and literature. The position is anything but comfortable as it continually alludes to its own ambivalences and enforces the ambiguity of transculturated discourse.

Xitu's introduction to *Maka na Sanzala* is quite fitting given the frequent repositioning of the narrator within the text. The narrative begins with the birth of a child in the house of Toko, a powerful sanzala quimbanda. The narrator soon interrupts this story, however, to interject another, that of Mafuta, Toko's much sought-after daughter, but not without warning the readers not to lose the first story line: "Esteemed readers, I find myself obliged to introduce you first to Mafuta and her Mafutas while old Kasexi is having breakfast at Toko's house. However, don't forget to tie the story's thread to this interruption when the time arrives."[23] The proper place appears eighty pages later. Thus the main body of *Maka na Sanzala* is devoted precisely to this narrative interruption. The link between the two stories, old Kasexi, appears in Mafuta's story only at its conclusion when the narrator again reminds the readers of the first story: "Perhaps the readers might remember old Kasexi from Botomona, who went one night to Calomboloca to old Toko's house to attend a birth."[24]

The narrator breaks into the story once again, not only to warn the readers of the different interruptions but also to comment on the language of the narrative. Toward the end of the first story when Kalutula and his friends appear at the administrative post because of their part in Mafuta's abduction, one of the sanzala elders delivers a diatribe against the breaking of traditional practices. In an aside, the narrator comments on the original linguistic register of the denunciation and his own narrative "reconstruction" into Portuguese: "This sermon was delivered in a Kimbundu so pure and in a tone so philosophical that it deserves a corresponding translation into Portuguese."[25]

The narrative commentaries draw attention to the diverse linguistic registers of the narration and point to an underlying Kimbundu narrative that provides the basis for the Portuguese one presented to the readers. The meta-textualizations also emphasize the hybridity of the transculturated narrative, in this instance, as the written textualization (*Maka na Sanzala*) of a story (Mafuta's) that exists in popular oral tradition.

Vozes na Sanzala also is set in the sanzala mainly in the 1930s. As was the case with *Maka na Sanzala,* this narrative combines supernatural aspects with elements of realism in its imagining of rural society. In particular, the detailed descriptions of local cultural practices are continually countered by those of imposed European culture, so that the vision of the 1930s rural village is that of a zone of contact with the Portuguese colonial presence. In this context, the elders blame the appearance of the Kasadi water spirit on the arrival of Christian missionaries and the resulting disrespect of the youth who dare to sing Christian hymns when they are bathing in Kasadi's waters.

Kahitu, the main character of the novella, is another of Xitu's imagined hybrid identities. He was disabled from birth, and the villagers attribute his condition to his parents' failure to fulfill a traditional obligation to the water spirit. As was the case of Tamoda, Kahitu is popularly called "mestre" due to his obsession with book-learning. As a child, Kahitu so identified with the *livro de João de Deus*—the traditional Portuguese pedagogical text—that he carried it with him wherever he went. Like Tamoda, Kahitu is self-taught, because his paralysis prohibited him from traveling to the distance school and the sanzala lacks sufficient funds to build its own facility. Because of his proficiency in Portuguese, Kahitu becomes the village translator and scribe, reading and writing letters for the inhabitants during regular office hours in his room. In addition, his role as mestre extends to the young unmarried adults who attend his classes as preparation for their roles in sanzala society. The mestre's situation is paradoxical, of course, for although he longs to *conhecer uma mulher* (be with a woman), the village mothers prefer that their daughters attend Kahitu's "school" rather than keep company with the city-influenced young men. Kahitu impregnates Saki and, rather than face judgment by the village tribunal, commits suicide. The narrative ends with the wrath of nature that seeks revenge on the sanzala for Kahitu's demise.

As in Xitu's previous narratives, the textualization of the seemingly traditional sanzala reveals a hybrid zone of ambivalent values. The villagers, for instance, revere Kahitu because of his supposed supernatural beginnings as well as for his knowledge of Portuguese that permits him to function as a type of cultural intermediary. Kahitu not only is the village scribe but also is responsible for educating the sanzala youth in the traditional ways. As Manuel Rui suggests, Kahitu represents a new hybrid element in the village society as a teacher, lawyer, and scribe.[26]

The tension between cultural elements in the sanzala is textualized in a narrative that combines conventions of orature and acculturated literature. *Vozes na Sanzala* uses mythological and supernatural elements, such as the apparition and the avenging force of nature, in a discourse that repeatedly

calls attention to its own literary structure. At one point the narrator interrupts the story of Kahitu and Saki to insert another story, that of Sange's
abduction. The readers are advised of the narrative switch just as they were
in *Maka na Sanzala*. The interpolation of another story incorporates the
meanderings of orature but in the context of written narration. Furthermore,
the fact that the narrator refers to this second story as the "the much talked
about case of Sange" intimates that the story is well known in the village
milieu. The ambiguity between legendary and oral elements of the narration, coupled with the repeated references to the literary narrative itself, is
underscored by the written homage—doubly written, that is, on both the page
and the tombstone—to Kahitu at the end of the narration: "Whether you
were born of a woman's womb or conceived in my imagination and born in
my head, I pay you homage by engraving this inscription on your tombstone."[27]
The ambivalence is underscored by a drawing of the tombstone, marked with
a cross but written in Kimbundu with a parenthetical translation.

The ending of *Vozes na Sanzala* with its hybridized tombstone makes as
much a self-mockery of Xitu's declared mission to preserve traditional cultures as his narrations do of the Portuguese civilizing mission. Xitu's narrations are mimicries of colonial discourse that play off the conventions of colonial representations and counter them through transculturated narrations.
The twist here, of course, is that Xitu is not only mocking the colonizer but
also his own attempts to preserve some pure, unhybridized, traditional form
of discourse. Kahitu is either born of traditional legend or is conceived self-
consciously by a fictional narrator whose self-reference is a commonplace of
modern European fiction.

In his mission to textualize the utopic precontact cultures of the rural regions, Uanhenga Xitu instead meets head-on with the ambivalent practices
of colonial contact zones, as should be expected. His public rhetoric aims at
the impossible, and his narrative practice simply demonstrates the futility of
an uncomplicated return to a mythicized source. Rather, Uanhenga Xitu narrates the pitfalls of colonial hybridity in a mocking and ultimately self-referential stance that questions his own transculturated narrations of colonial life
in the contact zone.

Resistance Novels and the Mimicry of Colonial Discourse

Uanhanga Xitu's novel, *Manana*, first published in 1974, also textualizes imagined cultural hybridity but moves the contact setting from the rural sanzala to
the colonial city. The oppositions of the earlier works—including rural/ur-
ban, past/present, and traditional/modern—converge in *Manana* to re-

create the immediate tensions of the urban contact zone. Once again, though, the surface dichotomies that would seem to propose a facile oppositionary stance are posed within the ambivalencies of narrative mimicry.

Xitu's mocking stance toward acculturated discourse that reveals a second position—that of the self-mocking narrator of ambiguous transculturated discourse—is partially revealed in *Manana*'s introduction. The first section, "Dedicatórias" (Dedications), contains no less than nine dedications that also present the text as a *livrário* instead of a *livro* (book): "But what is a *livrário?—Livrário* is like someone who spoke but didn't say anything."[28] The invention of the term *livrário* here poses the self-mocking stance of the author as an initial countering to European literary conventions.[29]

In *Manana*, Xitu appropriates the literary dedication for reasons of subversion, here through the exaggerated mimicking of its form. Further, while each dedication appears as an autonomous vignette that provides social background to the author's own hybrid formation in colonial Angola, all share a common emphasis on language, as evidenced by the first dedication: "To my friends from the shirt shops, the carpentry firms, the tailor's, the woodcutting firm, the shoe stores, the paper factory, the washerwomen, the vendors with baskets on their heads, the stone masons—all those I knew who didn't speak school-learned Portuguese."[30]

The elaborate dedications identify the conflicting sociolinguistic strata from which the languages of *Manana*'s discourse emerge: "You're all going to see: this *livrário* doesn't have fancy Portuguese. Nor school-learned Portuguese. Nor upper-class Portuguese. Nor functionary's Portuguese. Nor office Portuguese. It only has the people's Portuguese, from the neighborhoods, from the sanzala, from the village."[31] Xitu clearly announces that Portuguese models imparted through the various institutions of the colonial apparatus are rejected in favor of the nonstandard and creolized forms spoken in Angola. Thus linguistic registers marginalized within the dominant center of colonial society are moved from the periphery and given the status of literary languages, albeit here within the livrário. These marginalized registers imagine a collective identity that cuts across the surface boundaries of urban (*bairro*) and rural (sanzala, *quimbo*) sectors.

The specific choice of narrator, Filito, who is also the protagonist, provides the basis for the novel's exaggerated confessional form. Filito begins by narrating his childhood obsession to be a carpenter like his Uncle Chico. These aspirations run counter to those of his assimilado parents, who are intent on a more prestigious colonial social position for their son. But Chico opposes the position of his parents and points out the situation of assimilados who graduate from high school only to become colonial functionaries: "Their

life is to have shined shoes and a clean shirt. But at home they only eat man-
ioc with sugar. Even you, brother, have seen how many black graduates there
are. Only people from São Tomé are blacks with degrees."[32]

Chico, here the clearest voice of the people, discerns the pitfalls of colonial-style hybridity: the assimilado may have the formal appearances of the
colonizing class but back at home ends up eating just like the rest of Angola,
because assimilation is tightly controlled. Filito finishes school and at first
accepts a functionary position at the Tipografia but later follows Chico to
Uakua in order to learn carpentry. The main portion of Filito's narrative takes
place following his return to Luanda, where he has married, shares his house
with his mother-in-law, and works as a carpenter under the supervision of
mestre Joaquim, who is also recognized as a powerful quimbanda. The narrative recounts Filito's meeting with Manana and his attempts to establish a
relationship with her. *Manana* assumes the conventional pattern of marital
deception within the framework of a confessional narrative. However, the
convention is subverted through the ambivalent position of the narrator.

In order to secure Manana, Filito must proceed with certain rituals upheld by her traditional family. He acts accordingly but always with his own
motives of deception. Therefore while his immersion in the traditional sector
provides narrative space for the recounting of its cultural practices, Filito's
perspective is always ambiguous, particularly as he mimics acceptable traditional behavior. For example, at Rosa's birthday party, Filito, disguised as
Manana's suitor, moves easily between the traditional elders and the younger
adults. He first refuses to drink beer in front of the elders, but when he finally
accepts turns his back to them in order to watch the dancers. The elders in-
terpret his actions as respectful and declare him to be *"mesmo gente do respeito
e educada em casa da gente!"* (truly a person full of respect and brought up in
a fine house). Filito uses Kimbundu when he asks Manana to dance but immediately switches to Portuguese when he comments on his language and
formal behavior. His creolized description of two dancers, though, is more
revealing of his hybrid identity as he comments on the sensual movements of
the young women's *mbundas* (buttocks).

The chapter "A Minha Sogra!" focuses on the traditional funeral of
Manana's mother and the girl's own subsequent illness. Despite Filito's attempts to take her to a doctor, Manana's family insists that her condition is
provoked by spirits and sends her to a quimbanda in Funda to receive treatment. The following chapter, set in Funda, depicts traditional religious practices seemingly counterposed by a Protestant religious procession. Once again,
the cultural conflicts are disclosed through an ambivalent discourse whose
vision is that of hybridity: "The Protestants who sang 'Sivayá, Sivayá . . . ,' and

marching in a procession step, they acted as a class. And behind them many, many assistants. Taking advantage of the music that sounded so melodious and religious, some of them were shaking their buttocks to the drum beat."[33]

Once back in Luanda, Filito again fails to convince Manana's relatives to allow her to receive medical treatment. Her family insists that her illness is *da terra* (from traditional causes) and employs an argument not unlike that of the quimbandas in "Bola com Feitiço" who warned against mixing coisas da terra with colonial practices. They insist only a quimbanda can treat Manana and only after will they take her to the hospital. For his part, Filito realizes that he has lost Manana but blames the practices da terra while claiming that Christian values and teachings were unable to save her. In his review of the novel, Fernando Martinho argues that Filito's futile attempt to save Manana results from his own alienated position. He has broken with the traditional world but has nothing to offer it its place.[34] Even in death, Filito maintains that Manana is claimed by both the spirits and the sacraments.

Filito's self-representational narrative reveals the ambivalence of his own hybrid identity as he moves deceivingly through peripheries and centers of the colonial contact zones. The tension between the voices of implied author and narrator in Xitu's earlier texts openly manifests in the first-person narration itself. Fernando Martinho describes Filito as a conformist who accepts conflicting sociocultural exigencies in order to survive in the colonial formation.[35] Filito does seem to be a cultural chameleon of sorts who changes identities as he moves through different sectors of the contact zone. He mimics the traditional rituals during his deceptive courtship of Manana yet assumes a colonized identity in the institutions of the center, as evidenced by his business card: "Felito Bata da Silva, Joiner, Portuguese West Africa, Angola."[36]

The centers and peripheries in Xitu's works are never easily separated, so that if he claims in the exaggerated dedications to use the language of the collective "people," both that people and their language are themselves ambivalent. The hybridity of the assimilado is an easy target in Xitu's often farcical narratives, but it is that second glance into the mirror of hybridity, so to speak, that envisions the ambiguities of the peripheries. Manana's name, for example, is a case in point. This is a Kimbundu name, as emphasized in Filito's narrative, given to her as a baby by her grandfather. The priest reluctantly agreed to baptize her "Manana" but urged the family to call her Mariana or Ana.[37] Not surprisingly, Filito employs all three names throughout his narration, but this ambivalence is not his alone, as demonstrated by his inquiry in Funda: "I have come looking for a girl named Manana, also known as Ana, Mana Ana, Mariana, granddaughter of old Mbengu."[38] The girl's interchangeable names here appear as the confusions of her own hybrid upbringing in a Christian family that follows traditional terra practices.

Xitu's novel of hybrid identities in colonial Angola brings those peripheral ambiguities into the center of the author's mimicry. These voices are hybrid, often comically so, but it is from these hybrid registers that Angolan narrative speaks.

Os Sobreviventes da Máquina Colonial Depõem . . . (The survivors of the colonial machine testify . . .) is Uanhenga Xitu's first work entirely written and published after Angolan independence. As the title suggests, the novel is in part a work of resistance that testifies against Portuguese colonial exploitations and abuses.[39] As in Xitu's earlier narratives, the novel assumes the conventions of colonial literature—this time of the young Portuguese settler who seeks adventure and success in the *Ultramar* (the New State's designation for its overseas territories).[40]

Here, too, Xitu appropriates an acculturated literary model to write against convention. Therefore the story of José dos Anjos das Quintas e Celeiros do Rei, who responds to the State's open invitation to go to Angola and "continue the work begun centuries ago by heroes and brave men of the past for a greater Portugal," uses tactics that both mimic and subvert colonial novels of adventure.[41]

In contrast to the self-mocking tone of *Manana*'s classification as a *livrário*, Xitu in the introduction to the 1980 novel decisively places the problematic of Angolan literature in a sociopolitical context: "Literature is made by men who possess a great deal of academic baggage. . . . It happens that we, whose high school was in the settlements on the road, carrying sacks, picking cotton, splitting wood, and the pay given us was beatings and a kick in the behind by the colonial machine, and our University was the prison, therefore it's understandable that the most we can offer to readers are the images that we gathered during those years of direct observation of facts lived in the village, without being concerned with adornments and the style of fine Portuguese used by real writers. I am a writer of MULALA NA MBUNDA, mixing Portuguese, Kimbundu, Umbundu. We try to write in a way that can be understood by those readers who identify with our language and our way of life."[42]

Xitu's assessment of his literary practice with the Kimbundu phrase "mulala na mbunda," which, as Russell Hamilton explains, translates verbatim in Portuguese as "*pano folgado no cu*" and figuratively as "*escrevo no fundilha das calças*" (I write from the seat of my pants), might appear on the surface as a devaluation of his own writing.[43] Salvato Trigo, for example, views Xitu's assertions as an apology for this "deficient linguistic expression" and further suggests that Xitu thus excludes himself from an Angolan literature that he has helped to construct.[44] Obviously, Xitu's use of "literature" here is contextual and makes reference to the acculturated literary standards imposed by the máquina colonial. His supposed apology is really a contestation to the role that colonial literature has played in constructing images of the Portuguese empire. Xitu sets out to demystify those very images of colonization in the language and vision of those who participated in the less-than-heroic facets of the civilizing mission—brutal forced labor and imprisonment.

The author's introduction is self-referential as it addresses the ambivalent transculturated narration of the novel. Although *Os Sobreviventes da Máquina Colonial Depõem . . .* employs an implied authorial voice that provides an ongoing critique of the socioeconomic practices of the 1950s colonial regime, including forced labor, the educational system, and assimilation policies, the narrative assumes a quasi-bildungsroman form specifically associated with models of colonial literature. Thus a self-proclaimed survivor appropriates a literary form associated with the colonial machine as the basis for reclaiming historical vision and voice. Unlike Uanhenga Xitu's earlier narratives that counterpose an authorial voice to that of the narrator, the 1980 novel is narrated by an implied author who assumes the viewpoint of collective Angolan consciousness in terms of both political and cultural memory.

This collective perspective of the implied author is developed within a literary model associated with the neo-imperialist practices of the Portuguese New State. Beginning in the 1930s, the Salazar regime began to offer prizes for colonial literature through such institutions as the Agência Geral das Colónias and encouraged the creation of an ultramar literature. Although Xitu's novel simulates a bildungsroman fashioned in a quasi-colonialist mode, as mimicry, it also works toward the subversion of that same model. The narrative contains interspersed poems written by Uanhenga Xitu during his confinement in Tarrafal. These poems lament his imprisonment and exalt Angolan independence. The author again employs an exaggerated dedicatória that includes fourteen chronicle-like dedications to Angolans and Portuguese involved in the national liberation struggle.

This mimicry and subversion of colonial discourse involves a parallel disclosure of Portuguese colonialist ideology through a demystification of its images. The Lusotropicalist position of Portugal's nonracist Christian civilizing mission, based on that nation's prolonged contact with diverse races and cultures, is countered from the beginning of the novel. The Quintas e Celeiros do Rei family take pride in their historical association with the Portuguese monarchy—mocked in their extravagant name, of course—but the mother of one of José's classmates questions the purity of their genealogy: "For days now I've heard you say that the boy has blue blood. More likely its blood of the Moors or blacks, of the thousands of slaves who served the old kings."[45] The comment further demystifies the real basis of Portugal's historical contact with Africa as one of subjugation and enslavement.

Once in Angola, José encounters variants of the colonialist idiom utilized by officials and merchants as well as representatives of the Portuguese Catholic Church. His idealistic acceptance of the Portuguese civilizing mission is tempered radically by his daily experiences at the interior post, and he begins to question the ideology and practices of the colonial regime. José's criticism of the contract labor system and the role of the Catholic Church in enforcing colonial domination alienates him from the other Portuguese in the area. They suspect that José is conspiring with the American Protestant missions to encourage subversion among the African population and accuse him of maintaining contact with radical Portuguese. The time setting of the novel is important; it takes place in the early 1950s when the African colonies were officially changed from colony status to provinces in the face of mounting worldwide criticism. In the text, Portugal's renewed colonization appears threatened by the beginnings of organized nationalist resistance.

In its depiction of colonialism in the Angolan interior, *Os Sobreviventes da Máquina Colonial Depõem . . .* is reminiscent of the later works of Castro Soromenho,[46] in particular the trilogy *Terra Morta* (1949), *Viragem* (1957), and *A Chaga* (1970).[47] These three novels also are set in interior administrative posts and focus on the disillusionment, particularly on the part of low-level Portuguese administrators, with the dehumanizing practices of the civilizing mission. Although Soromenho's works are radical contestations to Portuguese colonial domination as well as to colonial literary models, they do not go beyond the social realist depiction of colonialism.

Xitu's novel, on the other hand, for all of its social-realist tendencies, moves beyond a merely critical stance in terms of political protests and the subversion of colonial discourse. The perspective of the implied author, informed by a collective political consciousness and cultural memory, imagines a demystification of colonial history.

Having demystified colonial discourse, whether in *Os Sobreviventes da Máquina Colonial Depõem . . .* or in the earlier narratives, Xitu proposes to textualize traditional cultural practices as a counter-discourse and an alternative history. Even in his 1990 autobiography, *O Ministro* (The minister—in the diplomatic sense), Xitu intertwines a fictional imagining of postcolonial Angola in his otherwise rhetorical memoirs. These imaginings also look to traditional practices as the heart of nation-space. The problem, of course, is that this counter-discourse is itself informed by the hegemonic strains of the colonizers, so that the discourse is necessarily hybrid. Xitu's narratives recognize that hybridity with a mocking double glance at both colonial discourses and counter-discourses. Having set himself to the task of recovering a pure counter-discourse, Xitu's texts demonstrate the impossibility of that task, as the counter-discourse has been formed in the contact zone. The mimicry, therefore, is always subversive, whether of acculturated literary languages and forms or the hybrid ones that have emerged on the margins of Portuguese colonialism.

Chapter 4

Visions of Utopia, Counternarrations of Nation

Forging the Nation

Homi Bhabha has described the liminality of the nation-space as that narration of selfhood that does not merely define itself in otherness, that is, in relation to other nations. Rather the narration of nation creates a liminal signifying space that deconstructs the monolithic construct of "we, the people" so that the imagined community is that of a heterogeneous, oftentimes contentious people.[1] These tense locations of culture in which dissonant voices of hybrid collectivity struggle to be heard are central to the narratives of Luandino Vieira and Uanhenga Xitu, but find their most explicit expression of nation as narration in the works of Pepetela.

Pepetela is the nom de guerre and the literary pseudonym of Artur Maurício Carlos Pestana dos Santos, born in Benguela, Angola, in 1941. He attended the Instituto Superior Técnico in Portugal as well as the Universidade de Lisboa, during which time he became involved with the Casa dos Estudantes do Império (House of students from the empire). Pepetela later studied sociology in Algeria where he was one of the founders of the Center of Angolan Studies. In the late 1960s, he returned to Angola and served as an MPLA guerrilla in Cabinda. After independence Pepetela was vice minister of education for several years and recently has worked at the Universidade Agostinho Neto. Pepetela's early works—*Muana Puó*, written in Algeria in 1969 but not published until 1978; *Mayombe*, written in the early 1970s and published in 1980; and *As Aventuras de Ngunga*, written in 1972—optimistically posit that the nationalist liberation struggle will transform contentious voices and histories into voices of a single nation. In these texts, differences of ethnicity, gender, region, race, class, and tribe are subsumed by the transformative master narrative of revolutionary socialism. It is not that these differences disappear or even that they become less tense, but rather that the utopian vision of nation resides in the praxis of the revolution itself. The violent negation of colonial identity, and with it the violent articulation of Angolanness, creates the liminal site for a hybrid expression of nation. There is a vision in these early works that the revolution itself will invent Angola from a space that was never necessarily nation.

Beginning with Pepetela's postindependence novel, *Yaka*, hope in the transformative power of revolution is increasingly questioned. Faced with the divisions that lead to continued warfare after independence, Pepetela turns to imagining the past in order to define an historical vision of collectivity. The textualizations of history in both *Yaka* (1984) and *Lueji* (1988) speak to the present ethnic, class, and racial divisions by offering collaborative visions of a past where boundaries of exclusion were crossed. Here the visions of utopia are located in a historical past that is inseparable from the imagining of future nation; the utopistic past of the protonation is what might lie immediately ahead.

What is missing from these postindependence texts is the narration of present nation as the dystopian space of disillusionment, discord, and despair. A *Geração da Utopia* (1992) narrates the collapse of utopia from the point of view of the generation that made the revolution in the name of nation. The novel textualizes the history of that utopic generation and its present configuration in a dystopian nation that has betrayed both praxis and past. In the disillusioned voice of one of the characters, the generation of utopia had hoped to build a nation in Africa but ended up building another African nation. Pepetela's most recent novella, *O Desejo de Kianda*, attempts to reclaim utopian and traditional space amid the disintegration of nation.

Pepetela, perhaps more than any other writer discussed in this book, questions the very construct of nation and the possibility of creating a common liminal space in Angolan narrative. It is somewhat ironic that the writer who most explicitly imagined the utopistic possibilities of both past and future nation-space narrates the present nation as a fractured space in which the boundaries of hybridity cannot be crossed. It becomes less ironic, however, if we think of Pepetela's narratives as forging nation, both imagining the hybrid spaces of liminality forged within revolutionary praxis as well as narrating the counterspaces of a divided community where the notion of nation itself is no more than a forgery.

Two MPLA guerrillas are lost in a dense wooded area. One ponders aloud, "How will we reach the Angolan nation?" The other responds, "Praxis, Camarada, praxis."

Pepetela's first published novella, *As Aventuras de Ngunga* (The Adventures of Ngunga), was written in 1972 as a pedagogical text for the reciprocal learning of Portuguese and Mbunda.[2] The novella bears comparison with Luandino Vieira's early works, *Vidas Novas* and *A Vida Verdadeira de Domingos Xavier*. All three works are somewhat didactic and focus on the transformations of identity through participation in the nationalist liberation struggle. In the case of Pepetela's narrative, the didacticism results in part from its original function as a literacy tool for both *pioneiros* (youth pioneers) and MPLA guerrillas.[3] All three are paradigmatic narratives in which individual stories represent the collective transformation toward national identities. In *As Aventuras de Ngunga*, the figure of the pioneiro attains a doubly symbolic status: Ngunga serves as a model for the present collective as well as for a new generation born of the tranformational revolutionary struggle. As the title indicates, the novella recounts Ngunga's adventures, the experiences that motivate the coming of age of an adolescent. The nationalist liberation struggle serves as the setting for this initiation passage so that the search for identity is twofold, for both adulthood and Angolan nationality.

The narrative of *As Aventuras de Ngunga* is set in the present and situated within the double transformational process of the armed struggle—that is, of rupture and reconciliation. This transformation in the present finds its dual basis in a critical examination of the traditional institutions and relations of the past that simultaneously questions the imagined nation of the future. Maria Mendes da Silva, for instance, divides the novella into three levels: the past, the present, and the future. She identifies the past with the novella's critique of traditional practices, whereas the present represents the construction of the *homem novo* (new man) with the future as his domain.[4]

The novella's critical examination of the past focuses on those structures or figures that impede the consolidation of national identity. However, the criticisms are formulated within Ngunga's simultaneous development into adulthood within the revolution and therefore assume the form of a search for appropriate role models who exemplify national identity. Certain structures, such as those that favor local group identities, are rejected in favor of models of nation. In addition, certain traditional practices, such as alembamento, are critiqued as contrary to the principles of the socialist revolutionary struggle.

The depiction of the pioneiro as a model for the revolutionary new man of the future is developed through Ngunga's experiences in various social sectors, including traditional villages, MPLA bases, the colonial prison, and the administrative post. Furthermore, Ngunga's critical questions are formed by these experiences and serve as the basis for his transformation as an adult and a revolutionary prototype. This transformation involves a movement from individual to collective values and further underscores Ngunga's representative status. Angolan writer Fernando da Costa Andrade has described Ngunga as a purely representational figure who is unreal as a person but who constitutes the intimate truth of every militant who understands the revolution as a universal dimension for the national definition of liberty, justice, and the new man.[5]

The narrative's paradigmatic function appears most explicit in the final section, "Para Terminar" (In closing), in which the narrator directly addresses the intended readers, namely the pioneiros and the guerrillas. The narrator first emphasizes that Ngunga's story is true and already exists in several oral versions, although certain details have been modified in the written narration. At the same time, the narrator raises the possibility that Ngunga might represent the necessity to transform shared by all of the camaradas: "Isn't it ultimately you? Isn't it in an unknown part of you yourself that the little Nugunga is modestly hidden?"[6] In this sense, the narrative proposes a collectivity that encompasses both readers and character within the self-representation of national identity. Ngunga's story, moreover, is already part of communal memory.

Pepetela's next published narrative, Muana Puó, was actually written in 1969 prior to As Aventuras de Ngunga, while the author was still in Algeria, but it was not released until 1978. Muana Puó appears as a radical break from the didactic tendencies of As Aventuras de Ngunga; but as Fernando Martinho notes, the two narratives actually combine the allegorical and the didactic so that even the more hermetic allegory of Muana Puó serves a didactic objective.[7] As Aventuras de Ngunga evokes allegorical aspects primarily through the use of symbolic figures and actions that represent the transformation of both colonial and traditional institutions and relations. In Muana Puó, allegory serves as the primary mode of literary representation and functions at several different levels within the discourse.

The text is divided into three parts—"O Passado" (The past), "O Futuro" (The future) and "Epílogo" (Epilogue)—which also correspond to three allegorical levels that Martinho terms "the collective, the individual, and the utopistic."[8] While Martinho certainly is correct in his identification of these three narrative levels, they are further interrelated within the separate sections, not only through the central figure of the mask—muana puó—but also through transformation. In addition, the novella's three sections and allegorical levels are unified within three different types of observation detailed in the epilogue.

Above all, *Muana Puó* is an allegory of collective self-representation that is imagined through the liberation struggle of the bats who have served as the divinely ordained slaves of the crows. The bats' struggle, moreover, is referred to as a search for light and not only involves a violation of laws but also leads to a demystification of the very basis of that sacred domination: "The bats understood then that God was an invention of the crows, with which they had always subjugated them in order to have honey without working."[9] The struggle leads to a parallel realization of the bats' real human condition. Obviously this allegorical level functions as a representation of the Angolan nationalist war with the demystification of Portugal's Christian civilizing mission. As in *As Aventuras de Ngunga*, the transformation involves the expression of a new identity within a future national community.

The second allegorical level marks the attempted reconciliation between the masculine and the feminine represented in the two bats—*ele* (he) and *ela* (she)—who participate in the struggle and ultimately become human. Their story follows a series of proximations and separations, and although the two never achieve a lasting union, the continuing search of the feminine for reconciliation provides the constructive basis of life and creation in the new social order. The search for definitive union is prefigured in the ambiguous gender identity of muana puó and its function in traditional Tchokwe rites when the mask of a meditative woman is donned by a male during rituals of dance.[10] Near the end of the narrative, the ele and ela meet each other in front of the mask and find a mutual recognition. The recognition is not of unity, though, as the two perceive the mask through a divided rather than totalizing vision. Moreover, the mask as artifact supports that approximate but divided vision, in that only through practice is a new identity assumed at that moment when the male dancer dons the mask of the woman.

Muana Puó's final allegorical level focuses on the construction of a utopian community, Calpe, following the victory of the transformed bats. This future, in which the means of production are collectively owned and goods are distributed according to need, is an imagining of a hybrid nation with fluid borders of identity. There is not so much a reconciliation of oppositions—individual/collective, masculine/feminine, past/future—as there is a fluidity of self-representation as figured explicitly in the fusion of antagonistic elements in the mask. The mask's totality is dependent on a totalizing vision that sees the whole but does not lose sight of the separate elements. This vision is a transformative one that encompasses the potentials of hybrid identities.

This totalizing vision marks *Mayombe* as the first Angolan novel to imagine the synchronic spaces of the nationalist liberation struggle.[11] Pepetela, working from a relatively simple story line that spans a short period of time, presents a comprehensive analysis of the historical moment that allows for the critical examination of specific conditions, policies, and practices within the nationalist movement.

Pepetela wrote *Mayombe* in the early 1970s while he was a teacher in Dolisie, an MPLA base in the Congo Republic. At that time, the MPLA Second Political-Military Region, which included the province of Cabinda and MPLA bases in the Congo Republic, was in a period of reorganization that had begun in 1970. MPLA guerrilla activity in the region had declined since the 1966–67 surge into the Eastern Front when many of the guerrillas in Cabinda were transferred to the new strategic sector. Pepetela has explained that *Mayombe* reflects the conditions in 1969–70, when a relatively small group of guerrillas were able to turn around the situation in the Second Region.[12] Although Pepetela was in Dolisie, both students and teachers participated regularly in military activities with MPLA guerrillas in the interior of Cabinda. The experiences, the difficulties of continued guerrilla activity, and the attempt to gain popular support in Cabinda during the extended period of impasse inform *Mayombe*'s narrative as a type of collective testimonial of the revolutionary struggle.

The novel's title refers to the dense forest region in the oil-rich enclave of Cabinda, a province separated from the rest of Angola that borders on Zaire and the Congo Republic. The theme of isolation in the forest region is intensified from the very beginning of the novel. Mayombe is depicted as an impenetrable, closed space, and if its seclusion provides cover from the Portuguese troops, it also intensifies the isolated conditions in which the guerrillas live and operate. Continual references are made to this separation throughout the novel, and in the context of the geographical distance, isolation functions at several levels. Indeed, Pepetela's working title for the novel was "Os Solitários de Mayombe" (The Solitary Ones of Mayombe). Only one of the guerrillas, Lutamos, (We Struggle) is a native of Cabinda; only he has intimate knowledge of the region, the people, and the Fiote language. Several guerrillas refer to the Cabindans as "counterrevolutionaries" because of the lack of popular support. Cabinda did have its own separatist movement, Frente de Libertação do Enclave de Cabinda (FLEC), which was active during the national liberation struggle. One of its leaders, Taty, even appears as a character in *Mayombe*. Regional and ethnic identities deepen in the isolated area, resulting in a threat to the unity of the guerrilla group.

This separation at the group level also is explicit in several of the individual militants who, for reasons of race, class, and lack of ethnic ties, see themselves as marginalized. Further, the relative inactivity of the guerrilla group creates a sense of isolation from the nationalist struggle itself. This is accentuated by the tenuous relations between the interior Cabinda base and the support base in Dolisie that is supposed to supply the guerrillas with provisions. André, the commander at Dolisie, is portrayed as an opportunist who uses his authority and the advance of the MPLA primarily to further his own position rather than to attend to the needs of the region. As a result, the Cabinda base lacks supplies, and new guerrillas are sent into the interior with neither adequate training nor additional provisions.

These various levels of isolation cause the guerrillas, as individuals and as a group, to question their actions as legitimate and representative of "an Angolan people." Unlike the Portuguese troops, they do not represent a recognized polity, and *Mayombe*'s narration of the nationalist war concerns the struggle for recognition of legitimacy as well as of national identity. Thus the conflicts among the various individual militants evoke the question of collective identity at the national level. Pepetela himself confirmed: "The real problem is national—what nation is this?"[13] The isolation—from the people, the movement, and the armed struggle—exacerbates divisions of region, ethnicity, race, and class and evokes the larger issues of Angolan nationness and collective identity. In this way, *Mayombe*, although focusing on a specific guerrilla group, depicts Angolan nationness from inside the potential transformations of the revolutionary struggle.

Transformations of revolutionary praxis are prefigured in the novel's dedicatory epigraph: "To the guerrillas of Mayombe/who dared to defy the gods/ opening a path in the dark forest/I will tell the story of Ogun/the African Prometheus."[14] Ogun, primarily known as the Yoruba *orisha* (deity) of war, is identified as the African Prometheus. Both traditional mythic figures divulge sacred knowledge to humankind; Prometheus gives fire, and Ogun shares the secret of forging iron. According to Yoruba legend, only Ogun with his ax of iron could clear the thick forestland.[15] Ogun is associated with the knowledge-seeking instinct, which Wole Soyinka also attributes to Prometheus: "Ogun is the embodiment of challenge, the Promethean instinct in man, constantly at the service of society for its full realization. Hence his role of explorer through the primordial chaos, which he conquered, then bridged with the aid of his science."[16] *Mayombe*'s evocation of Ogun as protector and the giver of force and intelligence to those who defy the gods provides an initial textualization of the liberation war; those who choose to open paths of defiance can persist only through knowledge and struggle. In this sense, the narrative's mythical transfiguration of Mayombe marks the tense space for the guerrillas' transformation through praxis.

The tensions of this liminal narrative space are posed by several narrative voices, representatives of the different hybrid identities that compose the heterogeneous, but potentially collective nation. These often antagonistic voices belong to the militants and appear at critical moments in the narrative. The use of different narrators opens the textualization of nation to a questioning of ideological motivations within the complex sociopolitical and historical context and at the same time permits a narrative self-representation of nation within a type of collective discourse.

The narrative voices are directed to the readers and specifically to Angolan readers who have shared in the experiences of the revolution. The subjective narrations are juxtaposed to events depicted through an objective narrative voice, and the questions posed by the militants often conflict with the actual events. The clearest example occurs in Milagre's (Miracle's) narrative passages in which he criticizes the punishment of another guerrilla, also of Kimbundu origin, who stole money from a Cabindan worker. Milagre addresses the readers to claim that Sem Medo (Without Fear), the commander, instigated the punishment because he is Kikongo and thus ethnically related to the Cabindan people. Milagre's accusation, itself motivated by ethnic, regional, and class ties, is contrary to the actual events: Sem Medo argued for leniency in light of the general lack of discipline within the region. The readers are forced to respond to Milagre's narrative, at least to the accusation that Sem Medo was behind the decision to punish the guerrilla if not also to deny the commander's supposed ethnic motivation. The various narrators' questioning provokes the participation of the readers and takes the attempt to create a collective narrative one step further to include the role of reception.

The first guerrilla to assume the narrative voice is Teoria (Theory),[17] the mestizo teacher at the Cabinda base: "I was born in Gable, in the coffee region. . . . I carry in me the irreconcilable and that is my motor. In a Universe of yes or no, white or black, I represent the maybe."[18] Teoria's ideological motivation has its basis in a questioning that will be repeated in other narrative sections—the boundaries of Angolan identity within a "nationalizable" area created by colonial domination. In Teoria's case, he is a maybe in the colonial manichaean world of rigid borders of identity. He volunteers for extra missions so that even the other guerrillas might forget that he is different and that he carries the original sin of a white father. Teoria may emphasize his ties to the Gabela region, but it is precisely the possibilities of hybrid identity that motivate his involvement in the MPLA: "I am in Mayombe in order to arrange a place for the maybe in the manichaean Universe."[19]

The question of ethnic alliances and divisions is introduced through the voice of Milagre, the Kimbundu *bazukeiro* (person who fires the bazooka). Milagre blames the domination of the Kikongos in the Second Region for its decline and questions what he is doing in Cabinda: "And we, those from the First Region, forced to fight the war here, in a strange region, where they don't speak our language, where the people are counterrevolutionary, and what are we doing here?"[20] Milagre's questioning, however, is viewed in light of his class origin and his experiences as well. He is from a peasant family and as a child in 1961 witnessed the massacre in his region by the Portuguese. In this context, Milagre also questions the right of Sem Medo, whom he describes as an intellectual alienated from the interests and experiences of the people, to judge the guerrillas' actions.

The ideological motivation of the intellectual is perceived most clearly in the narration of Mundo Novo (New World), the European-educated Marxist visionary who explains that he fights in the revolution because he is disinterested. But Mundo Novo is incapable of integrating theory and practice, regardless of the circumstances. He criticizes the *Comissário Político* (political commisary), for instance, for not immediately disciplining some of the guerrillas involved in an ethnically aligned argument, nor can he comprehend the reasoning that the dispute took place at a time when there was no food at the base.

The internal and interpersonal conflicts based on ethnic, racial, regional, and class differences are countered in the narration of Muatiânvua, a former sailor and son of an Umbundu father and a Kimbundu mother: "Where I was born, there were people of all languages living in the same miserable Company houses. Where I grew up, in the Benfica neighborhood of Benguela, there were people of all languages suffering the same miseries. The first group of children that I belonged to even had some white kids and many others born of Umbundu, Tchokwe, Kimbundu, Fiote, Kuanhama parents. . . . Today they want me to be a tribalist! From what tribe, if I am from all the tribes, not only of Angola, but also of Africa?"[21] Muatiânvua's motivations are class-based, formed from the shared sufferings of the DIAMANG company workers. He is incapable of taking sides in the Kikongo-Kimbundu conflict that threatens to split the command because his motivations are supraethnic, if not at times supranationalist.

These multivoiced narrative sections are complimented by the extensive dialogues and discussions that appear throughout the novel. These dialogues, especially between Sem Medo and the Comissário or Mundo Novo, examine organizational problems within the MPLA as well as the processes of national formation in a future independent Angola. It is through these dialogues that much of Sem Medo's character is revealed. Although he is the focal point of several of the other militants' narratives, Sem Medo never assumes the narrative voice. This may be explained by the fact that he figures predominantly in the dialogues and that much, but by no means all, of *Mayombe's* narration centers on his thoughts and actions.

The Comandante (Commander) first appears as an enigma; in fact his former nom de guerre had been Esfinge (Sphinx). He is described as the veteran of war and of men, who received his new name after singlehandedly holding off enemy soldiers so his base could be evacuated. His name in the story, Sem Medo, is somewhat ironic, as the Comandante fears death and most of all is afraid of this fear. Before each armed encounter he is haunted by images of Leli, his former lover, who died in 1961 in northern Angola while searching for him.

Sem Medo questions the possible political formation of a postindependence Angola and claims that in order to construct a socialist nation, discipline and party control must be tightened although inevitably the consolidations will result in hard-line bureaucratization. He criticizes those intellectuals who will not admit to their own intellectualism and who claim that a party actually dominated by their own class is composed of the proletariat. Sem Medo agrees with the goals of national liberation, nationalization, and agrarian reform but argues that this is neither socialism nor a proletarian state.

This questioning and criticism is perceived in light of Sem Medo's own contradictory formation. His primary value remains that of the individual, and while this allows him to discern the motivations and fears of the other militants, he is unable to adhere to a rigid apparatus that might restrict individual actions and thoughts. He is incapable of allowing actual practice to be translated into theory and in this regard counters the position of Mundo Novo. However, Sem Medo views his own role in the nationalist struggle as transitional: "I am the type who could never belong to the apparatus. I am the type whose historical role ends when we win the war."[22]

The character who comes closest to reconciling theory and practice is the Comissário Político. He is an intellectual of peasant origin who comes of age in *Mayombe*. His seemingly egotistical attitude throughout much of the novel is actually an attempt to camouflage his insecurities, especially in his personal relationship with Ondina, his fiancée, who is a teacher in Dolisie, and with Sem Medo. The Comissário's transformation is triggered by the discovery that Ondina has had an affair with André, the Dolisie base commander, and by the breakdown of his friendship with Sem Medo, followed by the latter's death. He narrates his transformation as the construction of a new skin that takes place in the context of a series of resolutions and advances in the Second Region. The ethnic conflicts in Dolisie that arise when a Kikongo (André) has an affair with the fiancée of a Kimbundu (the Comissário) are put aside in order to combat the common enemy. When the interior base is reported to be under attack, the mass mobilization in Dolisie is immediate and complete.

The transformations are evident also at the level of the other individual militants. Teoria intervenes in an argument between Kikongo and Kimbundu guerrillas without hesitation or fear. Lutamos realizes that his actions in the MPLA must serve as an example to the people of Cabinda as well as to other militants. Mundo Novo replaces André at the Dolisie base, and the fact that a seasoned guerrilla will head the support base implies an alleviation of the tension between the two bases. It is also implied that Mundo Novo's new responsibilities of resolving the day-to-day problems of the region will motivate his own transformation.

Sem Medo, too, is transformed, although this resolution is brought about by his death. Throughout the novel he is associated with the imposing solitariness of Mayombe, and in death he becomes mythicized as a hero, albeit a tragic one, in the voice of the Comissário: "Sem Medo resolved his fundamental problem: in order to remain himself, he would have to stay there, in Mayombe. Was he born too early or too late? In any case, not at the right time, like any tragic hero."[23]

The Comissário's narrative also serves as *Mayombe*'s epilogue. The questions and criticisms that inform the novel's contemplative imagining of nation-space are only partially resolved in the text. They remain central issues in the transformations of revolutionary praxis and the movement toward hybrid national identities. Although completed in 1971, *Mayombe* was not published until 1980, when it won Angola's National Literary Prize. Responding to a comment that the novel might be politically dangerous for those readers who incorrectly view Sem Medo as an ideal, Pepetela explained that the hiatus between the writing and the decision to publish was due precisely to the fact that the novel contained certain elements that, if interpreted incorrectly, might be potentially dangerous.[24] In my interview with the author, he emphasized that his doubts in 1978 regarding *Mayombe*'s publication did not concern the novel's questioning criticisms but whether the moment was appropriate: "if at the time the book couldn't be used by enemies of the MPLA when independence still had not been consolidated."[25] In spite of his preoccupations, Pepetela decided not to include an introduction to the second edition "because with an introduction, a part of the message of the book would be lost. That of making people think with their own heads."[26]

Back to the Futures

Pepetela's novel, *Yaka*, published in Brazil in 1984, is the author's first narrative work written after Angolan independence.[27] The novel moves away from the explicit narrative questioning of transformational revolutionary praxis to the textualization of Angolan history from 1890 to 1975. *Yaka*'s five sections follow a chronological progression—"A Boca" (1890–1904), "Os Olhos" (1917), "O Coração" (1940–41), "O Sexo" (1961) and "As Pernas" (1975)— and, as in *Mayombe*, provide a totalizing vision of the historical moments. The anatomical chapter titles refer to parts of *yaka*, a Jaga statue, and here the narrative progression also represents the statue's recomposition.

Pepetela's imagining of Angolan history is textualized through the saga-like story of the Semedo family, Portuguese settlers in Angola. Pepetela, of course, is not the first contemporary Angolan fiction writer to focus on colonial settlers. Luandino Vieira's 1967 novel, *Nós, os do Makulusu*, broke literary ground with its introspective, first-person narrative. Uanhanga Xitu's *Os Sobreviventes da Máquina Colonial Se Depõem . . .* also sought to demystify the ideological basis of Portuguese political and cultural domination through the mimicry and subversion of colonial discourse. On one level, the continuing history of five generations of Semedos corresponds to turning points in contemporary Portuguese domination in Angola. At the same time, these historical moments also represent the dates of African revolts in the Benguela region so that the saga-like history of the Semedos is counterposed by the parallel history of resistance and revolt culminating with the end of the liberation war and the subsequent power struggle between the three nationalist organizations.

The narrative of resistance is specifically introduced in the preface, in which the title's origin is explained: "*Yaka, Mbayaka, jaga, imbangala?* Were they really a social formation (?), Nation (?)—let the anthropologists clear that up. Creators of chiefdoms, assimilators of cultures, they formed armies with the young people of other populations that joined them on their journey, they seem only an errant idea, *cazumbi* spirit, in anticipation of nationality."[28]

The Jaga are identified as assimilators of cultures and a people whose continual struggle against colonial domination involved an alignment with other Angolan ethnic groups. Whether national or social formation, the Jaga prefigure the contemporary national liberation struggle and continue the focus in Pepetela's narratives on the question of a hybrid national identity. Unlike the previous works, however, the novel includes the descendants of Portuguese settlers in the national community, specifically those characters who assume Angolan identity and are aligned with the MPLA.

The two parallel historical narratives are related through the figure of the yaka statue. Like the muana puó mask, yaka appears throughout the novel as an enigmatic figure whose mystery can be deciphered only through a totalizing perspective. In this manner, the anatomical reconstruction of the statue corresponds to the development of the two interrelated histories. The Jaga statue, moreover, represents the assimilated artistic traditions of other Angolan cultures and thus becomes a symbol of nationness. The Jaga criticized Portuguese colonization ironically through their statuary, so yaka takes on anticolonial as well as national dimensions.[29] The statue's recomposition, alluded to in the chapter titles, implies the convergence of diverse groups within the context of collective national identity.

The first chapter, "A Boca" (The mouth), is set during the last years of the Portuguese monarchy. It begins in 1890, the year of the British Ultimatum that ended Portugal's claim to cross-continental territorial rights in southern Africa. The fourteen-year time span in this section incorporates the expansion and decline of the rubber trade in Benguela as a means to replace capital lost after the abolition of slave trafficking, as well as the beginnings of the British presence in Angola with the construction of the railroad in Lobito. The counterpoint to colonial history appears specifically in the figure of Mutu-ya-Kevala, known among the colonials as Quebra (Breaking), who attempts to unify several communities against the Portuguese. The next section opens with questions as to Mutu-ya-Kevala's whereabouts in the face of an increased colonial presence: "Where is he? The children even unlearned his name. There is no name that remains when the English train advances."[30]

The military expeditions carried out during the Portuguese First Republic and known in the colonialist idiom as wars of pacification, are reported through Tuca, an African soldier in the colonial army who describes the mass murders by settlers, the expropriation of lands, and the continued use of forced labor on the coffee plantations. This history of Portugal's increased hegemony of Angola may be told according to European chronology, but the perspective is that of the Other and runs counter to visions of pacification and territorial advances.

Yaka's third section focuses on the consolidation of New State policies in the colonies. Bartolomeu, Alexandre Semedo's son-in-law, involves the family in cotton production. After the "hunting incident" in which one of Alexandre's sons intentionally kills Tyenda and in turn is killed by Vilonda,

Bartolomeu takes advantage of the ensuing massacre by the Portuguese at Vilonda's *onganda* (homestead) to steal livestock and expand his holdings. Similarly in the fourth part, set during the 1961 outbreak of armed nationalist struggle, Bartolomeu identifies his neighbor, Noma, as a terrorist in order to seize his lands. His schemes continue during the factionalist fighting in 1975, as he joins all three nationalist groups in an attempt to retain his holdings in an independent Angola regardless of the outcome of the power struggle.

If *Yaka* evokes a model of acculturated literature, the novel simultaneously counters colonial historiography with a parallel imagining of African resistance, as well as through the antiheroic portrayal of the Semedo family that reads as a paradigm of twentieth-century Angolan colonial history. Óscar, the first Semedo settler, is a *degredado* (exiled criminal) who was sent to Angola for either political or criminal activities never clarified in the text. His son, Alexandre, the family patriarch, belongs to that group of Angolan-born whites referred to in colonial jargon as *brancos da segunda classe* (second-class whites).[31] The Semedo family's socioeconomic ascension from petty merchants to landholders is built on murder, exploitation, and deceit. Furthermore, Alexandre is the progenitor of another lineage that stems from a liaison with his African housemaid. His mulatto grandson, Chico, arrives in Benguela, mythicized as the mestiza city, but only Alexandre recognizes Chico's place in the family. The other Semedos embrace their mulatto relatives only at the end of the nationalist war in the hope that this racial mixing will serve as proof that the Semedos are Angolans rather than Portuguese. At the end of the novel, however, all the Semedos with the exception of Alexandre and his great-grandson, Joel, flee to South Africa in a convoy of trucks filled with Angolan coffee.

Portuguese colonial discourse is further countered through the characters' critical commentaries. For instance, Acácio, the anarchist barber who was exiled to Angola for political crimes, criticizes the Portuguese racist exploitation by both the monarchy and the Republic. His criticisms lead the other settlers to brand Acácio as a supporter of "savages"; indeed, the barber's unsolved murder seems motivated by his radical critiques of Portuguese colonial practice. Even Alexandre Semedo appears paradoxically as a colonial settler with a conscience, despite his obsession with obtaining a high socioeconomic status and his tacit compliance with Bartolomeu's ruthlessly exploitative methods. In spite of his wholehearted and vocal support of the 1917 Portuguese military expeditions, Alexandre later criticizes the passive acceptance of colonialist ideology: "We always were blind, weak people who wanted to fight back the storms with our hands. Believing ourselves to be heroes. Heroes of the sea, valiant immortal Nation. . . . Isn't that how our anthem goes? And we spread the Christian faith. . . . We only know how to recite memorized lessons. And the sad part is that we believe in them."[32] However, it is only at the end of the novel, with his choice to remain in an independent Angola and his support of Joel's decision to join the MPLA, that Alexandre assumes Angolan identity and finally comprehends yaka's mystery.

The countering of colonial discourse also incorporates an interweaving of narrative voices, although these voices are not as clear as those in *Mayombe*. The omniscient narration that establishes the chronological progression is counterposed by the first-person voices of various characters who often give stream-of-consciousness narratives. In addition to these voices, another distinct narrator appears specifically as a means of voicing continuing African resistance. This voice belongs to yaka and at times attains a register of collectivity that finds its basis in the statue's symbolic representation of revolt and national identity.

The counterposing narratives of colonialism and resistance converge in Joel's character as he assumes an Angolan identity, joins the MPLA as a FAPLA (part of the MPLA's popular forces), and fights during the 1975 struggle for power. The reconstruction of yaka's anatomical parts indicates a convergence of various groups within a collective national identity, but at the same time the novel ends in an open question, posed by yaka: "Well, now I can close these transparent eyes that have seen so many things. My creation is there in torrents of hope, the announced has arrived. I can let myself fall from the blow and remain in pieces on the ground, my mouth toward one side, my eyes toward the sea, my heart beneath the earth, my sex toward the North and my legs toward the South. Or is it better to still wait?"[33] This is a territorial marking of Angola, a setting of the boundaries, so to speak, of the tense locations of nation within the voice of narrative resistance. If the narrative remains open-ended, the question posed is one of continued resistance, however still within the borders of imagined nation.

In *Yaka*, the narration of historical resistance establishes a continuum of contemporary nationalism and, perhaps more importantly, speaks to the needs of the present and imagined futures. This is the history that has been displaced by dominant European historiographies intent on silencing resistance. If Pepetela reinvents that history, the intent is one of narrating an integral history of often contentious strains of resistance that may or may not become collective.

Pepetela's 1989 novel, *Lueji*, speaks of this project with more clarity than any of the author's previous works. Similar to the 1985 collection of short, interrelated texts, *O Cão e os Caluandas*, *Lueji* is set at the turn of the century.[34] But the imagined Angola of the near future is set against the past, as indicated by the novel's subtitle, "O nascimento dum Império" (The birth of an Empire). The empire here refers to the ascendancy of Lueji as leader of the Lunda and the difficult consolidation of her power. Lueji's four-hundred-year-old story is interwoven into the narration of the story of Lu, a dancer in Luanda's near future who is preparing to portray the Lunda queen in a dance performance that reenacts her rise to power. Their two stories first appear in marked sections, but as they become increasingly interwoven, the narrative switches turn more subtle, occurring even in mid-sentence, so that one is hardly alerted to the change. As Lu gets herself into character for her performance, the two women mesh, not in a depiction of magical-realist proportions but rather as a point-counterpoint in the dialogue between estória-história.

The estória in Angola is the narrative form that has become most identified with emergent Angolan national literature. First cultivated by Luandino Vieira, the estória is the tense, transculturated narrative that incorporates practices of orature and acculturated discourse. Central to the estória is the narrator-storyteller, whose narration is a performance of the particular text. The written narration is always one possible variation of the estória whose narrative threads are pulled and woven in one particular textual design. The other possible estórias remain an integral part of the configuration, waiting for the storytellers to weave new narrative patterns. Estórias are always about storytelling.

In Lueji, the question of how to "pôr a estória" (put the story) is most overtly developed in the interpolations of the narrator, the "I" who appears throughout the novel also as a character. In contrast to earlier Angolan estórias by Luandino Vieira and others, here the storyteller is clearly an escritor (writer) named Dinoluan.[35] Moreover, he is amoroso pela estória (in love with the estória) that Lu has scripted for her dance performance, and he wants to turn it into a novel.

The novel he writes is of course Lueji, with the added twist of further complicating the narrative levels. Lueji is the novel of writing a novel about the estória of writing an estória of a performance of a four-hundred-year-old história. At the center of the narrative tapestry is the conflict between the estória/história that manifests in the mirroring of the two women, Lueji and Lu, one of whom is essentially recreating the other through her estória.

As Lu sets out to write Lueji's estória, her overriding concern is to discover the truth of the história, so that the writing becomes a process of discerning the verdade histórica (historical truth) from the verdade estórica (truth of the estória). The reader of Angolan fiction cannot help but remember Luandino Vieira's estórias and the narrative search to discover the truth of the casos, a thread that has to be pulled so the estória must unravel its narrative. The verdade estória, however, always reveals the multiple levels and variations of the tale as a hybrid and collective narrative form. In Pepetela's text, Lu's estória realizes its own internal and artistic logic, but it is countered by the other conflicting versions of Lueji's história that have survived in oral histories. As one of the characters tells Lu, these conflicts are to be expected: "It's certain that there are contradicting versions. Like everything in oral tradition. Each group forms a version in function of its interests."[36] The novel incorporates Lueji's contentious histories in the narration of a collective history that is neither neatly put together nor always true.

The transformation of Lueji's história into Lu's estória runs the course of the inner novel and gives shape to the dialogue between história and estória. In the estória of the história, Lueji struggles against and ultimately breaks with the male-dominated Lunda traditions to become ruler when her father dies instead of her two older living brothers. She continues to bend Lunda tradition throughout her reign by forming new alliances and power bases as a means of creating empire. The Lunda empire, though, is in contrast to that other one of Portuguese making, so that Lueji's histories are resistant and also prefigure Angolan nationalism.

Mirroring her estória, Lu weaves her way through the intricacies of national culture in the Angola of the near future. In so doing, she learns the great lesson of Lueji's história, that identity, whether national or otherwise, is always negotiated within spaces of difference. As Lu attempts to negotiate her own identity as a contemporary Angolan woman and dancer, she turns to the legends and estórias of her grandmother in Benguela as well as to her grandmother's kimbanda, who invokes ancestral spirits and tells Lu to always think of Lueji. Like Lueji, Lu learns how to bend yet not abandon tradition, so that after the revolution the past remains meaningful for future actions.

Lu's negotiation of identity is paralleled in the estória that the artists bring to the stage of the Cine-Teatro Nacional as spectacle. Here the question is that of national dance and music as negotiated forms of collectivity. Lu's dance partners (and lovers) are part of this hybrid identity of the imagined future: Uli, from the island of Luanda (the Ilha), the son of a fisherman and a *kitandeira* who became rich through *candonga* (financial speculation) and who is graduating in medicine, and Cândido, an agricultural technician of Cuvale origin.[37] As the dancers perform the história of Lueji through the interventions of Lu's estória, history becomes physically present through the instrument of their bodies, and yet another version of Lueiji is created in the act of the dancing itself. This is the contemporary version that speaks to the interests of Angolan identity and imagines a hybrid nation where individual estórias are part of a common history.

The Generation of Utopia

A *Geração da Utopia*, published three years after *Lueji*, also textualizes the history of resistance, but this is the history of a dream deferred. The novel is divided into four chronologically marked sections and begins in 1961 with a chapter entitled "A Casa" (The house). The house in question is the Casa dos Estudantes do Império (CEI), the meeting place and cultural center for students from the African colonies studying in Lisbon. The group of Angolan students—among them Aníbal, the intellectual, who has written his thesis on colonial politics in the nineteenth century; Sara, of Portuguese descent and who is finishing her medical studies; Malongo, who is more interested in playing soccer than obtaining a degree; and Vítor, who is studying veterinary medicine—are trying to make sense of politics in Portugal and events in Angola.

The time setting is important, of course, as the students learn of the MPLA attack in Luanda and UPA attacks in northern Angola as well as the subsequent Portuguese retaliations.[38] In the months that follow, all of the students identify with the MPLA except for Malongo, who presents himself as apolitical, and Elias, who was educated by American Protestant missionaries in Angola and now supports UPA. Elias responds to Vítor's assertion that all Angolans must fight against colonialism without civilian massacres by calling Vítor's ideas "utopias." He further criticizes the students at the CEI who envision a multiracial Angola and advises Vítor and the others to read Fanon's writing on violence.

There is also a biting critique of the Portuguese left as being antifascist but not anticolonial. The May Day demonstration in Lisbon divides the Angolan students from their left-wing metropolitian counterparts who react as whites to the outbreak of armed nationalist struggle in Angola and who view all nationalists as terrorists. As Aníbal concludes, "We are the ones, with the war in Angola, who will overthrow fascism. This is the argument."[39] Aníbal, who has been drafted into the Portuguese army, deserts and goes underground on his way to returning to Angola in the ranks of the MPLA. The other students, including Vítor, Sara, and Malongo, leave Portugal for Paris and then for other destinations to study or return to Angola in the nationalist movements.

This first chapter sets the tone for the novel's historical vision. This is, after all, the Generation of Utopia who imagined a revolution that would counter criticisms such as those of one of the characters who claims that no revolution is like *os sonhos dos sonhadores* (the dreams of the dreamers). Sara's reply—"*Em Angola será diferente*" (In Angola it will be different)—identifies the expectations for the generation of 1961 as the utopistic union of national-ism and internationalism in a hybridized Angola.

This utopian imagining of nationness is rebutted in the three subsequent narrative sections, respectively dated 1972, 1981, and *"a partir de Julho de 1991"* (following July 1991). "A Chana" (1972) is set more than a decade into the armed struggle and is told from the perspective of Vítor, now an MPLA guerrilla leader whose nom de guerre is Mundial (Global). He has been sepa-rated from his guerrilla group and is wandering in the *chana* (bush) in the hope of finding the frontier. Mundial's reflections open the narrative space to the devastation of the war as the Portuguese massacre the civilian population of Angola. The deadly irony of the Christian civilizing mission is played out in the Angolan countryside as Mundial describes the planes with crosses painted on their undersides: "And there came the most Christian crosses of Christ, painted in red on the bellies of the bombers, dyeing the black bellies of the children a torn red."[40]

Mundial also recounts Aníbal's experiences in the MPLA as O Sábio (The Sage) and their conversation on regional divisions within the nationalist move-ment. Aníbal claims that he may come from the north but that his experi-ences in the war have deregionalized him: "I have lived in these woods for five years, I speak their language, I loved and totally respected a woman from the East whose death killed me. Am I really from the North? I never saw myself like that, I am only Angolan."[41] However, even he sees the change in the revolution as the guerrillas are no longer revolutionaries but rather more like mercenaries fighting someone else's liberation war.

Aníbal's disinterested self-representation as an Angolan is contrasted with Mundial's own opportunistic nationalism. Indeed after the revolution, in the chapter dated 1982, Mundial, once again Vítor, has become a Minister, and Aníbal, who had mentored him in the guerrilla movement, now labels him an opportunist. For his part, Aníbal has retreated to Benguela after leaving the army in 1977 and leads a somewhat solitary existence. He voices his disil-lusionment with the revolution as part of the Generation of Utopia and de-clares their vision of nation dead: "We thought that we were going to con-struct a just society, without differences, without privileges. . . . And afterward, everything became corrupt, everything rotted, way before we came to power. . . . The utopia died. And today it smells bad, just like any other putrefied corpse."[42] This is an Angola where the *candongueiros* (financial speculators) rule, and amputees wait years for prostheses.

By 1991, even the remains of the imagined utopia have disintegrated into what Aníbal had predicted would be *"o capitalismo mais bárbaro que já viu sobre a Terra*" (the most savage capitalism seen on Earth). This is the image of an Angola recolonized with the participation of the very generation that dreamed the utopian nation. Malongo has become wealthy as a broker for European businesses and in the eyes of his servant is worse than a colonizer: "That colonial is going to pay. These bosses come from outside and think they can rule us, that they can rob and beat us. The colonizer's time is over."[43] But the end of colonialism is denied in the narrative as Malongo's son-in-law claims that his own generation was already born impotent.

The new utopia does arrive in the person of Elias, the ex-UPA supporter who had gone to the United States and returned via Nigeria as a prophet of the Igreja da Esperança e Alegria do Dominus (The Church of Hope and Happiness of Dominus). Elias builds his church with the financial backing of Malongo and Vítor and damns the wealth of corruption from his pulpit. The churchgoers throw down their money and jewelry and leave the church in a carnival-like procession "*partindo felizes para ganhar o Mundo e a Esperança*" (departing happily to conquer the World and Hope). This is the new civilizing mission of the corrupt, a church used by the new post-independence ruling elite to preserve its own power and wealth while offering a false utopia to a recolonized Angola. While the rhetoric of the powerful has changed superficially, the relationship between the elite and the masses remains unchanged.

A Geração da Utopia does not mark a complete surrender to disillusionment and despair, for its non-epilogue refuses to put the final period to the narration of resistance and to the possibility of Angolan nationness. For all its questioning of the viability of nation within the contemporary relations of savage capitalism, the novel ends with a tentative note of possibility to an estória whose variations are yet to be told: "Obviously, an epilogue cannot exist, nor a final period for an estória that begins with therefore."[44]

Moreover, what is common to all of Pepetela's narratives is the sense that the novel may be finished for the moment, but the estória continues. Even in his most utopistic textualizations of nation, the narratives' questions admit the possibility of the failure of the nationalist revolution. In *O Desejo de Kianda*, published in 1995, Pepetela projects yet another utopian future, this time from within the failures of nation. In this short novella, Pepetela imagines the literal toppling of nation in the collapse of high-rise apartments built by colonizers but occupied by the revolutionary generation in the once-traditional Kinaxixi neighborhood. The buildings' collapse liberates the space buried beneath the asphalt of modernization and corruption, legacies of both the colonial and postcolonial regimes. This is a mythical space of desire, inhabited by the water-spirit Kianda, who ultimately succeeds in reclaiming a utopian territory from postcolonial colonizers of nation-space.

However, the reclaiming is on behalf of a traditional culture that is forgotten and invisible. The problem with Pepetela's latest narration of nation is that of his imagined traditional Angola. He cannot define the essential elements of that tradition, much less specify its particular concrete manifestations. History has, in fact, destroyed the remnants of traditional space and made some sort of hybridity the only possible reality. Pepetela alludes to this hybridity, particularly in the figure of Cassandra, the young girl-oracle who is the only character to hear the reemerging song of Kianda. Ironically, no one believes her, and the colonial/postcolonial walls come tumbling down. Pepetela cannot help but acknowledge the reality of hybridity, as he had done before in *Mayombe*; his prophetess of traditional Angolan space bears the name and plays the role assigned to her forebear in traditional Greek mythology.

More important, however, Pepetela's continual questioning extends even to the very viability of nationness in that tense, hybrid space of cultural difference. *Mayombe* may end in the optimistic voice of the transformed Comissário, but his epilogue affirms that the frontier between revolution and its betrayal is a fine line of sand in the midst of the desert, a line that places the borders of nation within the shifting desert sands that change over time. *Lueji*, as well, ends in an open question as to whether Angola as nation can survive its very hybrid identity, as Lu reminds us that even in reconciliation "*na ponta da flecha finca sempre uma gota de sangue*" (on the arrow tip there is always a drop of blood). Is this blood already spilled? Or perhaps, as I suspect, we are reminded once again that the map of the Angolan nation is tentatively drawn in blood.

Chapter 5

After the Revolution

The Irony of Independence

Euphoria and Irony

The three writers thus far discussed in this book began their imaginings of nation in the nationalist liberation movement and the armed struggle for independence. Luandino Vieira, Uanhenga Xitu, and Pepetela all assumed implicitly that the border crossing between colony and nation would mean a similar crossing between imagination and practice. Their narratives, in very different ways, textualize the hybrid collectivity of Angolan nationness as a form of liberation. Even in the most pessimistic of Pepetela's novels, a narrative thread is left hanging in the hope that the estória will be picked up where one history may end and be retold with another, happier ending. Although there are ironic elements in Uanhenga Xitu's texts of mimicry, for instance, irony is not the dominant narrative note.

Manuel Rui Alves Monteiro, who writes under his first two given names, was born in Huambo, Angola, in 1941. He earned a degree in law in 1969 from the Universidade de Coimbra, Portugal. In Coimbra, Manuel Rui was a member of the editorial board of *Vértice*, the literary journal of the Center for Literary Studies in which he published his first short prose works in the early 1970s. Following the fall of the Portuguese New State, Manuel Rui returned to Angola and served as the MPLA Minister of Information during the 1975 transitional government. Both a fiction writer and poet, Manuel Rui's 1976–89 annual publications of poems commemorating Angolan independence are collected in *Cinco Vezes Onze*.

Manuel Rui writes his most important narratives from a postindependence perspective, when the boundaries between colony and nation supposedly have been obliterated by the revolution. Like the other writers discussed in this book, Manuel Rui began with liberating imaginings of nation but in his case narrated from the initial euphoria of nationhood. This early imagining posits an Angola that finds its expression in the communal memory of the revolutionary struggles.[1] Collective identity in these early narratives is formed across tense differences of race, class, gender, generation, and ethnicity, but it assumes the common and euphoric language of nationness. Manuel Rui, more than any other contemporary Angolan writer, imagines nation using the modes of discourse that were created in the revolution itself. His textualizations of Angola are the euphoria of emergent nationness, and the new estória that will be passed on from generation to generation is that of the revolution.

The irony in Manuel Rui's early works, which is so pungently directed at colonial and neocolonial incursions into the struggle for nation, is tempered in these narratives precisely by the euphoria of independence. But beginning in the 1980s, this irony, once reserved for the "puppets of imperialism," finds uneasy targets in the imagined nation itself. Here the language of nation is turned upon itself in a mocking pastiche of revolutionary codes and slogans. The discourse of nationness has been betrayed in practice, and Manuel Rui's narratives respond to the betrayal with irony, and only irony. If the earlier texts countered the irony of the many colonialisms with the liberating discourses of revolution and nation, there was always the sense that these narratives were part of the lived experiences of all Angolans. The ironies of postcolonialism are also part of Angola's communal memory, but in the more recent works, that irony is not countered by euphoria. Rather the discourse of nation reveals a condition that is neither liberating nor hopeful.

Comrades in Collective Memory

Manuel Rui's first collection of prose fiction was originally published in 1973 while the author was still in Portugal. All five texts of *Regresso Adiado* (Postponed return) narrate the conflicts and contradictions of the metropolitan and colonial contact zones. Similar to the works of Uanhenga Xitu, here Manuel Rui is most concerned with the problematic of hybridized colonial identities, particularly in the narratives of assimilados on the margins of both societies. "Com ou Sem Pensão" (With or without meals), for instance, juxtaposes Armando Bernardo's expectations of life in the metropolis to the reality of his own marginalized position. In Angola, his status is defined in terms of the assimilated community: "He belongs to a class of well-dressed blacks who spoke good Portuguese and because of that he was called *calcinhas*."[2] Calcinhas (short pants) was the pejorative term for an assimilado. Now in

Portugal, as a student, Armando moves along the borders of his aspired community.

The story takes place following the outbreak of armed struggle in Angola, and Armando still adheres to the colonial concept of civilization even though he has always been marginalized from its center. Armando is no longer treated as a cross between *um homem e o animal de luxo* (a man and an expensive animal) because most Portuguese have relatives fighting against the African nationalists. As he searches for a suitable room in Lisbon, he repeatedly encounters antagonistic and racist reactions from potential Portuguese landlords. His entrance, or more aptly put, his lack of entrance into various households not only discloses the racism hidden within the civilizing mission but also reveals the real socioeconomic conditions of underdevelopment in the metropolis itself.

"Mulato de Sange Azul" (Blue-blooded mulatto) also narrates the alienation of the assimilado but this time in Angola itself. Luís Alvim, the title character, totally embraces cultural assimilation to the point that he embarks on a search to discover the noble Portuguese ancestry of his father. Alvim, therefore, rejects his maternal African heritage as well as his life as a *mulato benguelista* (a mulatto in Benguela) and opts for a petty administrative post in the Angolan interior. His death at the hands of Angolan nationalists is attributed to his attempt to reconcile the irreconcilable: "From having the blood of his father stand out from the indelible mixture with the blood that his mother inherited from enslaved people."[3]

Unlike Uanhenga Xitu's narratives of mimicry, Manuel Rui's early fiction sets out the conditions for undoing alienation, even in *Regresso Adiado*. In "Em Tempo de Guerra Não Se Limpam Armas" (Weapons aren't cleaned in time of war), Ribeiro Vintesete (Ribeiro Twenty-Seven), an African cook, and his younger friend, Mateus, pride themselves on their perceived acceptance into colonial society. However, their marginalized position is revealed when Ribeiro is attacked by a mob of white vigilantes in revolutionary Angola. In contrast to the other narratives of *Regresso Adiado*, the confrontation becomes Ribeiro's moment of awareness, and he arms himself with the weaponry of subversion. In the midst of the mob violence, Ribeiro saves himself by singing the Portuguese national anthem but removes his pants and defecates as he evokes the symbol par excellence of Portuguese nationalism and the colonial civilizing mission. Here the answer to alienation is the assumption of a new Angolan identity.

Ribeiro's reintegration is supported by the interpolative narrator who breaks into the story to address the readers regarding Ribeiro Vintesete's and Mateus's

Portuguese names: "Whoever thinks that Twenty-Seven and Matthew didn't have names before, incurs the serious historical error of someone who doesn't know that they did, but that these were ignorant names, black names, without music, without number, without Ribeiro or biblical verse Matthew thirty-something."[4]

The irony here is directed toward the culturally destructive effects of the civilizing mission and its institutions of domination. Although the narratives of *Regresso Adiado* contest the alienating conditions of Portuguese political and cultural domination, Manuel Rui's most significant contributions to an emergent Angolan literature appear after national independence, with the publication of *Sim Camarada!* in 1977. The estórias span the transition period from colony to nation, that is, from the formation of the provisional government to Angolan independence declared by the MPLA. These are the textualizations of the collective euphoria of nation amid the violent struggle for power during the period 1974–75. *Sim Camarada!* incorporates the cultural and linguistic innovations of this euphoria of nation as transculturating practices of narrative discourse. As critics of Manuel Rui's texts have argued, the language of nation is at the center of his literary practice.[5] The five estórias of *Sim Camarada!* are situated in the immediacy of recent history, but more important, they narrate this history as the collective memory of the emerging nation.

Sim Camarada! opens with a narration of the contradictory passage from colony to nation in the government formed by the Junta Governativa Portuguesa (Portuguese Governing Junta).[6] "O Conselho" (The council) follows a typical day of transitional governing with no attempt to disguise the identities of the various players. This is the ironic textualization of decolonization as the Portuguese High Commissioner daydreams throughout the council meeting of taking oil-rich Cabinda back to Portugal at the end of transition. The narrator further comments on the internationalization of the transition to nation: "The uninitiated reader should be aware that this was an international government. It had constituent parties. The Angola party, the American, the French, the Zairian, the German, and the et cetera parties."[7] In this sense, the transition to decolonization is narrated as a contemporary version of the Berlin Conference that authorized the division of Africa into colonial possessions. The division here, however, is of the emerging nation so that decolonization is expressed as neocolonization.

The various parties of the transitional government have their own specific codes of emerging nation, as is the case of FNLA Minister Graça Tavares, who addresses an MPLA minister as *mon frère*. The use of the French expression emphasizes the FNLA's links with Zaire and is countered by the MPLA's use of "camarada" as a term of socialist and internationalist orientation. In another instance, the slogan *poder popular* (popular power) attains real significance when an Angolan representative—and here it should be noted that Manuel Rui uses *angolano* as synonymous with the MPLA—argues that Tavares's proposal should be approved by vote and not acclamation. He receives the following response: "What? 'Augmentations' of 'people power' again? I think we ought to suspend the session for coffee."[8]

The contradictions of decolonization become all too clear to the Angolan people, however, as the transition from colony to nation leaves the boundaries of domination intact. "O Conselho" depicts a euphoria of nation that is tempered by the irony of transition. The estória may begin with this euphoria—"*o povo . . . com os olhos esbugalhados de independência*" (the people . . . their eyes wide with independence)—but as the passage to nationhood does not change the real conditions of the Angolan people, the stevedores and factory workers respond with strikes and demonstrations. In sharp contrast to the neocolonial sessions of the council, complete with porcelain and crystal serving dishes, cigars, and a white-gloved waiter, the Angolan people gather outside the luxurious palace, sit on the *bancos de desesperança* (benches of desperation), and watch the Mercedes cars come and go. As one *homem do povo* (man of the people) walks away from the palace with his hands in empty pockets, a friend stops to ask what he has been doing. He appropriates the code of emerging nationness and ironically replies, "*Transição*" (transition).

The language of the power struggle also is at the center of the emerging identity of nationness in "O Último Bordello" (The last bordello), an estória of the last remaining house of prostitution in a neighborhood that has been reorganized in the process of revolutionary struggle. The women in the surviving bordello depend on the FNLA and Zairian forces who have set up a base in the MPLA neighborhood, but their toleration turns to disgust and horror as MPLA militants and sympathizers are targeted by the FNLA troops. As the violence of transition continues, the women, countering the "puppets of imperialism," choose a new Angolan identity and come to be accepted as camaradas by the very MPLA organizers who had previously campaigned against them.

This taking of identity is played out in the linguistic power struggle, as one night the women refuse to serve four FNLA soldiers. When one of the women proclaims, "I'm not going to bed with any French speakers!,"[9] the drunken soldiers retaliate by killing several of the women and torching the bordello. Those who escape, including the aging madam, Mana Domingas, join a group of militants on their way to the MPLA-controlled neighborhood of Vila Alice to get weapons. The linguistic divide of identities is crossed as one of the militiamen asks angrily if the prostitutes have suddenly become camaradas. As the bordello burns amid the sounds of machine guns and grenades, Mana Domingas affirms her identity: "*Somos sim camarada*" (Yes, we are, comrade). This affirmation, which gives the collection of estórias its name, is underscored when Mana Domingas removes the gold chain given her by a Zairian commander and tosses it into the grass. She is armed, instead, with her crochet needle as she crosses the space between Avenida Brasil and Vila Alice, a space described in the estória as one of *vida ou de morte* (life or death). This is also the border zone between colonial identity and collective nationness into which Mana Domingas and the other surviving women take off their shoes and walk freely.[10]

The phrase "sim camarada" appears repeatedly in "Cinco Dias Depois da Independência" (Five days after independence) both as an affirmation of Angolan identity within the MPLA and as a means of collectivity across lines of class, race, and ethnicity.[11] The first part of the estória takes place in Luanda during the heated power struggle of the segunda guerra de libertação and ends five days after independence. The center of the estória is one of the pioneiro squadrons named for the fallen MPLA militant Kwenha, a group of children who assisted the FAPLA, the MPLA popular forces, in what is described as a serious game of life or death. One of these anonymous pioneiros protects a pregnant MPLA militant, Carlota, as they hide in a drainpipe during an FNLA attack.

The lines of solidarity formed between the middle-class woman and the poor pioneiro are embraced through the mutual use of "camarada" as a term to overcome the boundaries of class prevalent in colonial society. In this sense, the narration of the party attended by the *"pequena burguesia do EME "*(petite bourgeoisie of the MPLA) assumes a critical tone but also textualizes the diverse composition of the nationalist movement as it crosses lines of class and race. The unity is in the common struggle against neocolonialism and is expressed through the shared language of nation: "The language was highly codified. 'Imperialism,' 'neocolonialism,' 'puppets,' 'lackeys,' 'people power' were all terms that rolled off every tongue."[12]

This shared code of nationness forms the narrative basis of common memory in "Cinco Dias Depois da Independência," set in the midst of the violent confusion and rapid progression of events on the eve of Angolan independence. Carlota searches for the unnamed pioneiro and is repeatedly criticized by other militants who remind her that the nation is in jeopardy and there is no time to waste on individual cases of heroism. No one will listen to the story of the fearless pioneiro until Carlota encounters a soldier doing guard duty on Independence Day—a captive audience, so to speak—outside the MPLA building where she hid with the young boy. Her estória of the pioneiro is, of course, the narration of the nation as the sun rises on the first day after Angolan independence. It is the estória of a child who may or may not have really existed, but whose story is the collective emergence of nation in the figure of the representative pioneiro as the image of Angola, past, present, and future.

In many ways, "Cinco Dias Depois da Independência" is the estória of a collective estória of nation, the common memory of revolutionary struggle and an independence challenged from its very beginning. In the imagined figure of the pioneiro, the estória becomes a vehicle for the difficult narration of nation. Difficult in the sense that the narrator of "O Conselho" poses with the critique of those who naively believed in a facile transition from colony to nation and that "the page of history had in fact been turned. All that had been necessary was to lick your fingertip, place it on the page, and flip it over!"[13] *Sim Camarada!* textualizes precisely that difficulty in turning the page on colonial history and proposes, instead, that the narration of nation is necessarily a collective project that really can never be adequately written.

"O Relógio" (The watch), however, is just that collective narration of an estória of nationness and once again centers on the role of children in imagining Angola. A further affinity is established with "Cinco Dias Depois da Independência" in that this is essentially the estória of an estória and in this case involves the Sunday-afternoon storytelling sessions led by a disabled MPLA guerrilla commander. The commander, who assumes the role of a griot, tells the tale of a watch taken from a Portuguese major killed in a skirmish and then exchanged to a Zairian patrol for the lives of MPLA guerrillas. Each week, the estória is transformed through the active role of the commander's audience—children who ask questions, change details, and thus retell the tale as collective authors.

The narration of "O Relógio" cultivates the tension between literature and orature through the use of such terms as *repaginar* (repaginate) and *reescrever* (rewrite) in the context of the oral storytelling session. The use of such ambiguous terms is underscored by the assertion that no author would be able to put the many versions of the oral estória into writing. This is an estória, like those of Luandino Vieira, that ends but does not conclude, as it is part of common memory. The estória's transculturated form is contrasted, of course, through the tale of the watch as a metaphor for the European sense of time. Here the purpose of the watch is subverted, as it is traded for the lives of nationalist guerrillas. More important, however, the European sense of narrative time is challenged in the counternarration of *estória* that does not measure time with a watch.

This is a positing of narrative time that does not have precise borders of measurement but rather is compared to the movement of the sea from which the commander draws his inspiration. This sea, moreover, is bordered by a children's beach, a space of future imaginations of nation and possibilities of collective authorship. Images of the sea figure repeatedly in Manuel Rui's prose fiction and poetry from his earliest works to the present.[14] The author has emphasized the significance of the sea in his works as a symbol of what he terms *mudança estática* (static change): "The sea is something always equal and always changing."[15] In "O Relógio," the sea is given to the children by authorization of the revolution and signals their own authored participation in the complex and changing narration of nation.

The sea also functions as a central image in Manuel Rui's 1980 novella, *Memória de Mar* (Memory of the sea). The figure of the sea, as a symbolic synthesis of permanence and movement, is signaled by the citation from Manuel Rui's poem "Mar Novo" (New sea): "Nothing remains that is not part/of the necessary change./So speaks the sea."[16] *Memória de Mar* describes the expedition to the Ilha dos Padres (Priests' Island) by a historian, a sociologist, and the first-person narrator-chronicler. Their voyage is dreamlike and passes through various time periods with the initial setting being *dois anos depois de quinhentos*, or two years after the end of the five-hundred-year Portuguese presence in Angola. The group finds the island mysteriously deserted and moves back in time to the last year of Portuguese domination to decipher the mystery. Here the dreamlike aspect of the expedition is countered by the narration of the power struggle among the three nationalist movements and their international allies, as well as by the preponderance of historical elements taken from the five hundred years of Portuguese colonialism. *Memória de Mar* traces not only the written chronicle of a specific voyage but also the historical and collective memory of Portuguese domination.[17]

This latter aspect appears most explicitly in the figure of the Portuguese submarine submerged off the coast of Luanda during the 1975 power struggle. The officials on board are anticipating a combined FNLA-UNITA victory in order to demonstrate in Portugal "in that which was the great betrayal of April 25."[18] The submarine is only the latest Portuguese sea vessel to embark on voyages of colonization; it lies in wait as the present-day caravel of neocolonialism. This function is underscored by the diverse historical figures who mysteriously appear in the submarine, including the Viceroy of India with his retinue of noblemen and priests. This appearance at the end of Portuguese colonialism evokes its beginnings as the Viceroy announces his presence in early sixteenth century Portuguese: "Sirs, the King by order of his grace, commands that we impose our faith upon the infidel and our civilization upon the heathen who in return must pay the insignificant and material tribute of cinnamon, gold, and ivory."[19] Here the submarine is also the convergence point of the various colonial myths, from the non-economically motivated Christian civilizing mission to the technological aspects of Portuguese and international neo-imperialism.

The historical elements of *Memória de Mar* are counterposed by fantastic figures and events, such as the Quitanda water apparition that destroys the priests' stronghold. The siren clearly is representative of African cultural resistance that ultimately participates in the final demise of Portuguese colonial hegemony. In addition, the burros on the island, similar to the bats in Pepetela's *Muana Puó*, are transformed once they identify with the revolutionary struggle. Although they do not become humans, the burros find their own voices of collective identity. The double meaning of the *burro* in Portuguese is important—both a pack animal and an uncouth person—as a means of invoking the Portuguese colonial categories of "civilized" and "noncivilized" as well as the transformational aspects of revolutionary practice.

The expedition members encounter the abandoned submarine and its artifacts but leave them behind at the bottom of the ocean as part of the colonial past. Rather than return to the present, the group travels to a imagined utopian future in which the Ilhas dos Padres has become the Ilhas dos Pioneiros (Island of the Pioneiros). The novella ends with the return to the present, and the narrator's true function is revealed as that of designating the historical time and place of the written narration as Luanda, February 1978. The narrator's hesitation to date the chronicle—"*o ter de assassinar o maravilhoso com a insônia do tempo*" (the having to assassinate the fantastic with the insomnia of time)—is the reluctance to impose the mark of European historiography on a counternarration to dominant Portuguese discourse.

If *Memória de Mar* evokes European historiography, it does so as a means of subversion and a countering to the chronicles of discovery that also oftentimes recounted the dreamlike voyages of the early explorers. This is a different chronicle of nationness, though, as the final mark of date and time underscores. *Memória de Mar* depicts the expedition of an independent Angola, and as a counterpoint to the chronicles of colonizing discoveries, it chronicles those discoveries that are liberating and transformational within the possibilities of nation.

Pigs, Dogs, Rumors, Kites: The Irony of Nation

Quem Me Dera Ser Onda (If only I could be a wave), published in 1982, signals a radically different narrative perspective from that of either *Sim, Camarada!* or *Memória de Mar*. The collective euphoria of nationness, so vividly textualized in the earlier *estórias*, is contrasted in *Quem Me Dera Ser Onda* and Manuel Rui's subsequent texts by the ironies of independence, as the line separating colony and nation grows fainter by the day. Here the colonial boundaries of class, ethnicity, and generation are redrawn in configurations of nation, so that the narrative is filled with revolutionary ghosts who talk the talk of emerging nation but walk along the lines of colonial boundaries.

Quem Me Dera Ser Onda is set in postindependence Luanda, a city transformed from the collective battleground of nation to one of daily survival. Amid the food shortages, endless lines, telephones and elevators in disrepair, assaults, and labyrinthine bureaucracy, a family decides to raise a pig for slaughter in their apartment. The two children, Ruca and Zeca, though, adopt the pig as their pet and unsuccessfully try to prevent its death. Within the novella's ironic vision of nation, the children appropriate revolutionary *palavras de ordem* in their campaign to save the pig.[20] In one instance, they criticize two of the building's *responsáveis* (responsibles) for both misspelling and incorrectly using revolutionary discourse in a notice prohibiting swine in domestic dwellings: "Excuse me, comrade Nazario, but swine is with an *s*, discipline is before vigilance, and in front of the struggle continues you have to put by means of Popular Power and at the end finish with year of the founding of the People's Assembly and Extraordinary Party Congress!"[21] Ruca later writes a composition for school about the pig in which he calls his father "bourgeoisie and reactionary" because he won't eat fried fish like the common Angolan people. The pig, on the other hand, is deemed revolutionary and must be saved as part of the struggle of the *pioneiros* against a generation that does not know the palavras de ordem.

Quem Me Dera Ser Onda explores the ironies of daily survival from the collective perspective of nation. Expressions that are related to Angolan life experiences are interspersed throughout the novella, frequently with humorous intent. The term *peixefritismo* (fried fishism) for instance, satirizes the overuse of *ismos* (isms) in the revolutionary society. The inspector who shows up to inspect the family's apartment is labeled a *faccionista* by the children, a reference to the bloody 1977 putsch by a splinter faction of the MPLA. Similarly, the father's reference to one of the *responsáveis* as a *"catete da merda"* (shit from Catete) evokes the past MPLA political rivalry between militants from Catete and the urban intelligentsia.

Even the pig's name — *carnaval da vitória* — assumes important significance in common memory as a sign of cultural resistance. The Portuguese colonial regime had banned African carnival celebrations during the period immediately preceding the outbreak of armed nationalist struggle. The first celebration after Angolan independence was known as the *carnaval da vitória* (carnival of victory). This reference also evokes Agostinho Neto's famous poem "Havemos de Voltar" (We must return), written while the MPLA leader was imprisoned in Portugal in 1960 and which includes a verse concerning the prohibition of carnival: "To our carnival/We must return."[22]

If the language and images of nationness are evoked in *Quem Me Dera Ser Onda*, the intent is one of irony, as the pig whose name ressonates with the struggle for political and cultural liberation becomes somewhat of a *reclassé*. Even the somewhat westernized father criticizes the pig: "*Estás a aburgesar*" (You're becoming bourgeois). The pig eats leftover food collected from the garbage bins at the luxurious Hotel Trópico, is bathed daily with imported Brazilian soap, and has its own headset with which to listen to the national radio station. The image of the pig is the irony of the revolution several years into nation; the euphoria of the victory carnival has been ruptured by the contradictions of nation. The rhetoric of revolution and nationness remains but is ridiculed in the figure of the revolutionary pig, who despite his bourgeois tendencies is the most devoted listener of national radio.

Quem Me Dera Ser Onda's ironic imagining of nation bears comparison with Pepetela's 1985 work, *O Cão e os Caluandas* (The Dog and the Caluandas).[23] In the Pepetela work, too, the struggle for daily survival is revealed through the ironic manipulation of the rhetoric of nationness. *O Cão e os Caluandas* is composed of short texts — newspaper articles, diary entries, interviews, plays, letters, official reports, and plays — linked by the mysterious figure of the German shepherd who turns up in various areas of Luanda and, even more mysteriously, in other parts of Angola. The dog's wandering adventures in Luanda are recounted by different narrative voices to provide a totalizing vision of nation in the 1980s that includes food lines, excessive bureaucracy, *candonga* (financial speculation), abuses of power, and the vestiges of ethnic and racial animosities.

O Cão e os Caluandas' multivoiced narrative opens the text to the ironic use of revolutionary rhetoric, most explicitly in "Tico, o Poeta" (Tico, the poet). The title character uses *palavras de ordem* to justify his refusal to work, as he is an intellectual revolutionary. Similarly, Tico explains that the German shepherd, a breed once owned only by whites and associated with the colonial order, has become *proletarizado* (a member of the proletariat). When the dog abandons Tico, however, that same language of revolution becomes the vehicle for the ironic vision of nation: "The scoundrel was really a lumpen, sat down to lunch, slept, woke up and went on with his life. Without saying goodbye. A parasite, an exploiter. And I, Tico, a revolutionary intellectual, didn't write that poem that I had thought about. The sacrist didn't deserve it, he retained the bourgeoisie mentality, enemy of the worker-peasant class that I belong to, exploited for five centuries."[24]

In *O Cão e os Caluandas*, the irony of independence is offset in the future positioning of the implied author. Although the official reports, diaries, interviews, and so forth date from the mid-1980s, the supposed publication date of the text is 2002. This distancing imagines a future Luanda as a utopian space in which the revolution has been realized. Indeed the new Luanda is designated as Calpe, the utopian city established after the revolution in Pepetela's earlier narrative, *Muana Puó*.

Quem Me Dera Ser Onda also contrasts its ironic interpretation of nation, albeit not with the imagining of a future utopia, as is the case also with *Memória de Mar*. Here the counterpoint is in the figures of the children who appropriate the rhetoric of revolution, which is quickly becoming moribund, and breathe new life into the language of nation. The pioneiros in *Quem Me Dera Ser Onda* are those who try to save the pig and the revolution from the ironies of independence. They dream of setting the pig free by the sea and imagine themselves to be the fast and furious waves that paint the sea with the unlimited possibilities of nation.

The ironic vision of nation continues in Manuel Rui's later narratives, *A Crónica de um Mujimbo* (The chronicle of a rumor), published in 1989, and *1 Morto & Os Vivos* (1 corpse and the living), published in 1993. In the former, the path of the *mujimbo* opens the narrative to the critique of nation, particularly in the figure of Henrique Feijó, a high-level functionary.[25] Feijó is caught in the bind between colony and nation as he laments the passing of colonial Luanda with its clubs, cabarets, and *fado* houses.[26] In contrast to the nostalgic colonial high times, everything in the neocolonial nation is in disrepair, and what is left over is consumed by foreigners who leave clutching Angolan dollars. This is the neocolonial nation in which colonial life is paradoxically replicated.

Feijó's life is a compendium of the ironies of neocolonial Angola. A former revolutionary, Feijó in the postrevolution develops a taste for all the material trappings of the bourgeoisie, even as the material situation worsens in Angola. His wife Joana, for example, complains bitterly about the food shortages in Luanda but not from the perspective of the masses of Angola's people who wait for hours in food lines. Rather, she bemoans the lack of special fruits she needs to comply with her new weight-loss regimen. The Feijó family vacations at the beach, taking with them the fruits of neocolonialism—Adidas, bermuda shorts, and "ti-xartes" (T-shirts). Yet Feijó and his coworkers blame all of Angola's problems on that very neocolonialism of which they partake. When they learn that Feijó's office is infested with "colonial rats" (the rats date from colonial times), office staff members attack the *desratizadores* (exterminators, literally "de-ratters") as foreigners who take Angolan money for killing rats. This is the North-South dialogue of the new world order: "Technology transfer. Know how. New international economic order."[27]

If the rhetoric of revolution has become empty in Feijó's mouth—he defends the cooperatives but obviously buys his own goods outside of Angola or on the black market—and the promise of nationness represented by that discourse is the site of a new colonialism, that irony is offset by the mujimbo. Here the mujimbo represents a counterdiscourse of nation that finds its force through popular oral tradition. As one of the characters explains, in a nation in which the masses are illiterate and cannot afford radios, they are dependent on the mujimbo as a means of connecting their experiences to the collective. The mujimbo, then, is the oral form of common memory that resists the controlled mechanisms of officially sanctioned discourse. Furthermore, as a collective form of narrative, the mujimbo, like the traditional tales, can be told and retold by all members of the community. In this sense, Manuel Rui's *Crónica de um Mujimbo* is not concerned with the content of the actual mujimbo, for indeed this probably changes in the individual telling, but rather with the telling itself as a creative collective act. Like the estória of the watch, it is the telling of the story that narrates nationness, regardless of the configurations of each individual tale. Here, the mujimbo is an act of resistance, only this time to a nation that has been recolonized in the name of liberation.

This irony deepens in "O Rei dos Papagaios" (The king of kites), from Manuel Rui's collection, *1 Morto & Os Vivos*. The king of kites is a young boy named Kalakata whose ear has been burned off in a fire caused by a petroleum lamp. Kalakata is mocked by the other musseque children and rarely chosen for games, and spends most of his time outside of school waiting in the food lines to get bread for his family. What saves Kalakata is his passion for art; he makes sculptures and toys from discarded materials. He even gains a measure of fame among the other children on account of his majestic kites, made from the scraps of paper found at the National Press. As his fame grows, he is commissioned to make kites for two boys who live in the wealthy section of Luanda. These are the children of a judge whose job is, in the words of Kalakata's father, to *"defender-nos da bandidagem"* (defend us from banditry).

Of course, as the narrative reveals, the judge fails to defend Kalakata or even recognize his humanity. Kalakata's kites, made from luxurious foreign materials brought back by the judge from his travels, win prizes and bring Kalakata momentary fame as he is interviewed on a national children's radio program. After being temporarily held up as an exemplary *pioneiro* of the new Angolan nation, Kalakata finds himself back in the food lines in the musseque, where one afternoon he is beaten and robbed of his family's ration card and his bread. In the confusion that follows, the judge passes by in his official sedan and stops to inquire about the robbery. He is told that this is just another *"maka dos gregos"* (argument among the marginalized lumpen poor), and he leaves without recognizing Kalakata or intervening on his behalf to catch the thieves.

This failure of recognition is, in a sense, the failure of the revolution that had promised to erase the colonial barriers of class by creating a common Angolan identity. The judge, whose job it is to protect this common identity by enforcing equal justice, refuses to intervene when the quarrel is merely among those who are dismissed as gregos. His perception of the marginalized is a nonperception, a nonrecognition of their humanity. It is not that all gregos look alike, but that all of the poor can easily be dismissed as gregos.

The last scene of the *estória* is reminiscent of an earlier Angolan tale. Kalakata returns home to the wrath of his mother, who blames him for the loss of his family's ration card, the only legal way of obtaining food in Luanda. His cry at the end of the *estória*, *"Mama, eu não sou grego"* (Mother, I am not a grego), echoes the ending of an *estória* written thirty years earlier by Luandino Vieira. In "Vavó Xixi," the title character's grandson is stripped of his iden-tity, labeled a terrorist, and whipped by a Portuguese merchant. The grandson defends his innocence and in his protest is an implicit counter-assertion of his Angolan identity. He is not what the Portuguese colonizers label him but rather what he might become through the experience of the revolution.

Thirty years later, after the revolution, Manuel Rui's character Kalakata makes a similar protest, this time against the label placed on him in the neo-colonial nation by the new ruling elite. Ironically, the term for a marginalized lumpen who lives by thievery is grego, also Portuguese for "Greek." The term strips the lumpen of their nationality, even of their race, and imposes a foreign identity on their peripheral positioning. Kalakata's denial then, is actually his assertion of Angolanness and of his right to be included in the nation. Thirty years after *Luuanda* and the narrative reconquest of Africanized space, that territory has been relinquished to a new colonization, and the demarcation of the city into separate, class-divided sectors has remained inviolate. Kalakata may cross over from the musseque to the home of the wealthy judge. He can even eat at the judge's table with his children and make them kites. He cannot, however, be recognized as a human being once the barriers of neocolonialism have been recrossed.

And so the narrative of nation has come full circle. For Manuel Rui, the future imaginings of nation have always been expressed in the promises of a new generation of pioneiros who are authorized to narrate the nation by re-telling the estórias of revolutionary and national euphoria. These are the estórias betrayed by Feijó, the judge, and a new ruling class that made independence but not a nation. For Manuel Rui, the only hope of nationness is in the hope that the pioneiros of *Sim Camarada!, Quem Me Dera Ser Onda,* and "O Rei dos Papagaios" will complete the promises of the national liberation struggle and imagine a true revolutionary nation. For the moment, however, the revolution has eaten its children when the children of Angola cannot eat.

Chapter 6

Narrations of a Nation Deferred

The initial project of the Angolan writers discussed in this book was to imagine a nation where no nation existed in the political sense. That imagined nation was rooted in part in traditional practices, narrative and otherwise, as well as in an ideologically based construct of a socialist revolution that would transform the colonial formation into a utopian postcolonial Angola. When history deferred those dreams, these narrators reacted either by retreating into silence, like Luandino Vieira, into self-parody, like Uanhenga Xitu, or more creatively, into an ironic posture that stopped short of despair, like Pepetela and Manuel Rui. Pepetela, in particular, kept alive a dream of nation that would arise from the ruins of the revolution but could find no compelling new metaphor for that imagined nation. Manuel Rui's vision was ultimately more bitter and at times seemed to abandon all hope that the revolutionary generation could save the revolution. Hope could be found only in the children of Angola who were themselves the new narrators of nation.

The dilemma faced by these writers is by no means uniquely Angolan. The vision of nation arising out of traditional forces transformed by the power of generally Marxist ideas was common to many of the literatures of colonial Africa. What good was it to throw off the yoke of the colonial oppressors if there was no promise of a better postcolonial future? The intellectuals' task was to construct that future by defining those elements that made for a national culture, those traditions that would and should survive into the postcolonial utopia, and to provide for an ideological framework to place those national revolutions into the internationalist strains of socialist ideology.

That project always contained contradictions. By constructing what was uniquely national, these visions necessarily clashed with a Marxism that posited a universality of social conditions and a revolution that was transnational. Those contradictions did not have to be resolved so long as the nation or nation-building focused on the concrete goal of independence. Moreover, those underlying historical conflicts between classes, social groups, ethnic loyalties, and regional ties could be imagined away as merely products of colonialism that would end with the exit of the colonizers. This imaginative project thus wished away the uncomfortable and potentially divisive elements of difference in the dreams of unified and leveled nation. The struggle against colonialism would forge unity out of difference and a single nation out of a history of division that in many cases predated the advent of colonization.

History, however, defeated imagination. In fact, in Angola and elsewhere in Africa, the advent of independence did not create nation but in many cases exacerbated divisions. The Angolan civil war, in that sense, was not unique at all. How to deal with the impingement of reality on imagination was a task not only of Angolan writers. The reactions of those Angolan writers are also representative of strategies of postcolonial narrations amid the deferred dreams of nation.

Be that as it may, for all the common ground that one can find in post-colonial African narratives, Angolan writers stand somewhat apart in that their imaginings of nation always raised the possibilities of a dream deferred by divisions of class, ethnicity, race, political alliances, and regionalisms. These narratives that date from the 1960s to the mid-1990s took into account the lessons of other new African nations as well as those lived and learned in the fighting fields of Angola itself. The protracted nature of the Angolan revolution gave pre-independence Angolan literature a more complex sense of the difficulties, if not improbabilities, of nationness. Those pre-independence narratives are informed by the doubts and ironies created by historical experiences of postcoloniality not usually present in the literatures of revolutionary struggles, which tend toward simplistic socialist realism.

The two decades of ensuing civil war have only deepened the ironies of imagined nation. In this respect, too, Angola's postcolonial experience has been perhaps more openly bitter, tragic, and yet ignored. If it sometimes seems that the combatants in that civil war have forgotten what they are fighting for, the narrators of Angola have at least tried to keep alive, in however attenuated a form, the possibilities that the revolutionary struggles were worth the candle. History may yet prove that dream to have been not only deferred but an illusion.

Notes

Preface

1. Gerald M. Moser, *Essays*, 1.
2. Barbara Harlow, *Resistance Literature*, 85–86.
3. Frantz Fanon, *The Wretched of the Earth*.

Chapter 1. The History and Context of Contemporary Angolan Narratives

1. See, for example, James Duffy's analysis of "The Congo Experiment" in *Portugal in Africa*.
2. Gerald Moser includes both the original text and the English translation of a 1540 letter from Afonso to King John III of Portugal (61–63).
3. Eduardo de Sousa Ferreira, *O Fim de uma Era*, 137.
4. For an insightful study on the failure of the Portuguese *colonatos* (agricultural communities) see Gerald Bender, *Angola under the Portuguese*, chap. 4.
5. Duffy, *Portugal in Africa*, 204.
6. See Mário António, *Luanda, "Ilha" Crioula*, for an analysis of creolized cultural patterns.
7. Russell Hamilton, *Literatura Africana*, 36.
8. Américo Boavida, *Angola*, 31.
9. Gilberto Freyre, *Portuguese Integration in the Tropics*.
10. Perry Anderson, "Portugal and the End of Ultra-Colonialism," 113.
11. Duffy, *Portugal in Africa*, 53.
12. Ibid., 126.
13. Douglas Wheeler and René Pélissier, *Angola*, 130. All references are to chapters written by Wheeler.
14. Ferreira, *O Fim de uma Era*, 141. In addition, Gerald Bender reports that 44.2 percent of the white population in Angola in 1950 had no formal schooling (248).
15. Gerald Bender, *Angola Under the Portuguese*, 151.
16. Ferreira, *O Fim de uma Era*, 157.
17. Gerald Bender, *Angola under the Portuguese*, 153.
18. Ibid., 204

19. Basil Davidson, *In the Eye of the Storm*, 149. See also Henrique Abranches, *Reflexões sobre Cultura Nacional*, 35–36. Abranches details the commercialization of traditional African culture and the transformation of its art into *objectos de luxo da sociedade de consumo* (luxury items of the consumer society).

20. Wheeler's chapter on the *Estado Novo* or New State is called "Discovering Angola, 1925–61."

21. This latter discovery refers to the theme of *Mensagem* as "Vamos Descobrir Angola" (Let's Discover Angola). Mário António (Fernandes de Oliveira), one of *Mensagem's* collaborators, refutes this slogan in "Memória de Luanda (1949–1953)." *Mensagem* (1951–1952, four issues, the last three published in one special number) was published in Luana by the Departmento Cultural da Associação dos naturais de Angola (Cultural Department of the Association of Naturals of Angola). Angolan collaborators included Agostinho Neto, Mário Pinto de Andrade, Mário António Fernandes de Oliveira, and Viriato da Cruz

22. Wheeler, *Angola*, 96.

23. Joaquim Cordeiro da Matta was a self-taught historian, philologist, journalist, and folklorist. In 1891 he published *Philosophia popular em provérbios angolanos* (Popular philosophy in Angolan proverbs). See Russell Hamilton's *Voices from an Empire*, 26–31. Hamilton also includes the later António Assis Júnior in this group and discusses his 1934 novel, *O Segredo da Morta*, as a chronicle of creole society.

24. Wheeler, *Angola*, 126–27.

25. There were actually four numbers of *Mensagem*, but the last three were released in a combined issue.

26. The journal by this name is not to be confused with an earlier *Cultura* also published in Luanda between 1945 and 1951.

27. Hamilton, *Literatura Africana*, 35–36.

28. Amílcar Cabral, *Unidade e Luta*, 227–28.

29. Gayatri Spivak, "Can the Subaltern Speak?" 271–313.

30. Barbara Harlow, *Resistance Literature*, 82.

31. Mary Louise Pratt, *Imperial Eyes*. In her first chapter, Pratt examines practices of transculturation in the contact zone. Pratt's usage of the contact zone will be more fully developed in my third chapter.

32. Quoted in Ferreira, *O Fim de uma Era*, 148–49.

33. Abranches goes so far as to say that "we have on our hands a bipolar cultural heritage." *Reflexões*, 105.

34. Agostinho Neto, *Ainda o Meu Sonho*, 17.

35. See Russell Hamilton's analysis of acculturation and acculturated literary practices in the Angolan nationalist era as put forth in *Literatura Africana*, 22. Hamilton argues that acculturation practices that reinforced exploitative domination can be transformed by members of the dominated group into arms of liberation.

36. Edward Said, *Culture and Imperialism*, 209.

37. Harlow, *Resistance Literature*, xvii.

38. José Luandino Vieira, "Canção para Luanda," 239–41. The poem was originally published in *Cultura* (II), no. 1, in 1957.

39. Ella Shohat, "Notes on the Post-Colonial," 99–114.

40. Benedict Anderson, *Imagined Communities*, 7.

41. Homi Bhabha, *Locations of Culture*, 113.

42. Frantz Fanon, *The Wretched of the Earth*, 51.

43. Bhabha, *Locations of Culture*, 4.

Chapter 2. Countermapping Luuanda

1. For a detailed account of Luandino Vieira's activities during this period see Michel Laban's interview with António Cardoso, "Encontro com a Literatura Angola."

2. Russell Hamilton, *Voices from an Empire*, 57.

3. Gerald Bender, *Angola under the Portuguese*, 223.

4. Salvato Trigo, *Luandino Vieira*, 206.

5. José Ornelas, "José Luandino Vieira," 61.

6. Stuart Hall, "Cultural Identity and Diaspora," 222.

7. Michel Laban, "Encontros com Luandino Vieira," 71.

8. Trigo, *Luandino Vieira*, 210.

9. Russell Hamilton, *Literatura Africana*, 131.

10. Tractores invejosos a soldo de bandos de inimigos desconhecidos invadiram-nos a floresta e derrubaram as árvores. Luandino Vieira, *A Cidade e a Infancia*, 62. Unless otherwise noted, all translations are my own.

11. De todos nós, meninos brancos e negros que comemos quicuérra e peixe frito, que fizemos fugas e fisgas e que em manhãs de chuva deitávamos o corpo sujo na água suja e de alma bem limpa íamos à conquista do reduto dos bandidos do Kinaxixi. Luandino Vieira, *Cidade*, 66

12. Luandino Vieira, *Lourentinho*, 11–71.

13. Quando eu era o teu amigo Ricardo, um pretinho muito limpo e educado, no dizer de tua mãe? Luandino Vieira, *Cidade*, 92.

14. Manuel Ferreira, preface to *Cidade*, by Luandino Vieira.

15. Triste vida a do mulato Armindo! Mas quando ele contava até parecia bonita. Parecia aquelas histórias do cinema. Luandino Vieira, *Cidade*, 158.

16. Contarei agora a história do Faustino. Não foi a Don'Ana que me contou, não senhor. Esta história eu vi mesmo, outra parte foi ele mesmo que contou. Luandino Vieira, *Cidade*, 139.

17. Luandino Vieira wrote *Vidas Novas* in 1962 in the Cadeia Central da Pide in Luanda, where he was imprisoned awaiting trial on charges of political activities against the New State. Clandestine editions circulated prior to official publication in 1975.

18. Salvato Trigo refers to the story-within-a-story form as a *"narrativa bifronte,"* 382–83.

19. Então vou pôr a estória de Cardoso Kamukolo, sapateiro! Luandino Vieira, *Vidas Novas*, 97.

20. See Héli Chatelain, *Folktales*, 254–55, on the traditional opening of the missosso.

21. *Luuanda* has been translated into English by Tamara Bender with the same title. All English translations of *Luuanda* come from that version and are indicated by page number in the endnotes.

22. Isto é que possa ser contada por outro e manter um fio que é o que a identifica, para cada um poder fazer variações com aquilo. Luandino Vieira, interview with the author, July 16, 1985.

23. Chatelain explains that "the reduplication indicates repetition of the act. The meaning is the sum as that of the habitual *ngene mu ta*, or *ngeniota*, i.e., I am wont to tell, am in the habit of telling, I often tell." *Folktales*, 254.

24. Uma coisa que já foi contada e que agora estou a contar e que será novamente contada. Luandino Vieira, interview with the author.

25. Tamara Bender's translation, 44. From Luandino Vieira, *Luuanda*, 70: O papagaio Jacó, velho e doente, foi roubado num mulato coxo, Garrido Fernandes, medroso de mulheres por causa a sua perna aleijada, alcunhado de Kam'tuta. Mas onde começa a estória?

26. Bender's translation, 46. From Luandino Vieira, *Luuanda*, 72: É preciso dizer um princípio que se escolhe; costuma se começar, para ser mais fácil, na raiz dos paus, na raiz das coisas, na raiz dos casos, das conversas.

27. Bender's translation, 46. From Luandino Vieira, *Luuanda*, 72–73: Então podemos falar a raiz do caso da prisão do Kam'tuta foi o Jacó, papagaio mal-educado, mesmo que para trás damos encontro com Inácia, pequena de corpo redondo que ele gostava, ainda que era camuela de carinhos; e na frente com Dosreis e João Miguel, pessoas que não lhe ligavam muito e riam as manias do coxo.

28. Hamilton, *Literatura Africana*, 131.

29. Chatelain, *Folktales*, 306.

30. Bender's translation, 109. From Luandino Vieira, *Luuanda*, 153: Minha estória. Se é bonita, se é feia, vocês é que sabem. Eu só juro não falei mentira e estes casos passaram nesta nossa terra de Luanda.

31. Hamilton, *Literatura Africana*, 131.

32. Laban, "Encontros com Luandino Vieira," 51–52.

33. Um rio parece é uma vida de pessoa, verdade mesmo. Luandino Vieira, *Velhas Estórias*, 167

34. O Makutu, um rio; rio, a vida do Kanini, rios correndo no separado juntos. . . . Os rios davam encontro o mar das muitas mais águas. Luandino Vieira, *Velhas Estórias*, 169

35. Trigo, "O Texto de Luandino Vieira," 247.

36. Se é bonita minha estória, se é feia, vocês é que sabem. Luandino Vieira, *Velhas Estórias*, 214.

37. Os casos que vou pôr, passaram na esquecida noite de 11 de Março de 1938, no Makulusu, naquele tempo nosso musseque. Luandino Vieira, *Velhas Estórias*, 193.

38. E foi a última vez que passaram casos de quinzar no Makulusu, naquele tempo nosso musseque e hoje bairro-de-branco. Luandino Vieira, *Velhas Estórias*, 224.

39. This novel has been translated into English by Richard Zenith as *The Loves of João Vêncio*. All English translations come from this version and are cited by page number in the endnotes.

40. Este muadié tem cada pergunta! . . . Porquê eu ando na quionga?

41. Zenith's English translation, *Loves*, 1–2. From Luandino Vieira, *João Vêncio*, 33: Dou o fio. O camarada companheiro dá a missanga—adiantamos fazer nosso colar de cores amigadas.

42. Zenith's English translation, *Loves*, 64. From Luandino Vieira, *João Vêncio*, 118: Este muadié tem cada pergunta! . . . : missangas separadas no fio, a vida do homem? Da de maria-segunda, de cada cor, cores? Kana ngana! Cada coisa que ele faz é ele todo—cada cor é o arco-íris.

43. In my personal interview with Luandino Vieira, July 25, 1985, he stated that he made up this song but in the style and language of popular songs of the period.

44. Hamilton, *Literatura Africana*, 217.

45. Casos que estão já na cantiga, são casos de pior confusão—poeta mussequense sempre é dono único de suas verdades mais diferentes. Luandino Vieira, *Macandumba*, 57.

46. Ora, na cantiga puseram: "araracuara foi entrar na quionga"—ou no português do estado: o polícia deu entrada nos calabouços prisionais. Exageros mussequentos, vê-se logo-logo a lição das estórias ensina. Luandino Vieira, *Macandumba*, 57–58.

47. E como assim, casos de meter brancos, tudo parece é o jogo de miúdos de musseque: monte d'areia vermelha; lá no dentro um fio enrolado à toa; se puxa-se malem-belembe caem os paus de fósforos espetados. Luandino Vieira, *Macandumba*, 57.

48. The reference here is to a comment made by Luandino Vieira in one of our July 1985 discussions in which he described the impact of orality on the literary as "the total freedom to invert paths." Luandino Vieira, personal interview, July 25, 1985.

49. Para poder pôr a estória, primeiro pergunta-se saber: o próprio—Pedro Caliota, na mundélica ignorância assimilado para Iscariotes—quem que quis de muquila fazer viola, adiantar uns casos só passaram ainda em estória de missosso, no antigamente? Luandino Vieira, *Macandumba*, 13.

50. Voltando nos casos: Caliota, pobre pedro ou moisés morto nas águas, quem que pensava era imortal em sessenta-e-um? . . . Mas para começar outra estória pergunto saber: pessoa pode morrer só, morto malsassinado num dia de todos os sóis? Luandino Vieira, *Macandumba*, 52

51. Edward Said, *Culture and Imperialism*, 216.

52. Barbara Harlow, *Resistance Literature*, 85.

53. See Carlos Ervedosa, "Cartas do Tarrafal," 85–88, on the events surrounding Luandino Vieira's arrest en route to exile in England, as well as on the novel's manu-script.

54. Luandino Vieira, "Acho Que Já Trabalhei Um Bocado," 8.

55. Pires Laranjeira, "Luandino Vieira," 358. He identifies the chapter sequence as 2, 1, 4, 3, 5, 6, 8, 9, 7, 10.

56. A narrativa da vida de Domingos Xavier não só permite compreender o grau de mobilização e de integração das camadas sociais no combate nacionalista, como esclarece também, através dos diversos diálogos, a sua natureza e o seu conteúdo. Mário Pinto de Andrade, "Uma Nova Linguagem," 223.

57. Carlos Vieira Dias, better known as "Liceu," was one of the legendary figures of contemporary Angolan culture. With his musical group, Ngola Ritmos, Liceu, who died in 1994, was in the vanguard of Angolan cultural revindication.

58. Qualquer lutador e de qualquer patriota que em circunstâncias análogas vive. Maria Lúcia Lepecki, "*Luandino Vieira*," 134

59. Os teus amigos sabem que estás preso e confiam em ti, te mandam bilhetes com palavras de coragem, precisas cumprir, Domingos Xavier. É verdade, irmãos, preciso de cumprir. Luandino Vieira, A Vida Verdadeira, 72.

60. Verdade, mano Liceu verdade. Você ainda não está no fim, todos estamos contigo em tua prisão. . . . O Ngola toca tuas músicas, o povo não esquece, mano Liceu. Luandino Vieira, A Vida Verdadeira, 159.

61. Laban, "Encontros," 38.

62. Mais-Velho's name literally designates his place in the family as "the older one." His brother is "Maninho" or "little brother," here being the diminutive of the Portuguese mano. Their mulatto half-brother is referred to as "Paizinho" or "little father," thus indicating only his Portuguese heritage.

63. Simples, simples como assim um tiro: era alferes, levou um balázio, andava na guerra e deitou a vida no chão, o sangue bebeu. Luandino Vieira, Makulusu, 3.

64. Trigo, Luandino Vieira, 601.

65. See Donald Burness, Fire. Burness claims that Maninho is an MPLA guerrilla and that Paizinho, the narrator's mulatto half-brother, is the father.

66. Laban, "Encontros," 37.

67. Libambos de escravos, libambos de mortos, de presos, de contratados, libambos de homens livres—toda uma história a desenterrar. Luandino Vieira, Makulusu, 80.

68. Harlow, Resistance Literature, 85–86.

69. Russell Hamilton, "Black from White and White on Black," 51.

70. Isto, Mais-Velho é que é difícil e tenho de o fazer: o capim do Makulusu secou em baixo de alcatrão e nós crescemos. E enquanto não podemos nos entender porque só um lado de nós cresceu, temos de nos matar uns aos outros: é a razão da nossa vida, a única forma que lhe posso dar, fraternalmente, de assumir a sua dignidade, a razão de viver—matar our ser morto, de pé. Luandino Vieira, Makulusu.

71. O teu relativo vira absoluto meu—solidariedade, é assim?—e vai também me tranquilizar, nascer a certeza que depois vou destruir e destruindo-lhe para lhe reconstruir e ir assim, contigo que não és tu mas nós, os do Makulusu, fabricando, não a certeza, mas certezas que vão nos ajudar a ser nem cobardes nem heróis: homens só. Luandino Vieira, Makulusu, 130–31.

72. A vida não é o tempo, é sua memória só—já o esquecemos e queremos é chegar ao século vinte e um. Luandino Vieira, Makulusu, 81.

73. Nós não usamos a língua portuguesa porque alguém nos dê autorização, ou por estatuo, ou por requerimento, or por esmola. É um troféu de guerra. Luandino Vieira in Carlos Vaz Marquês, "Luandino," 9.

74. Tamara Bender, preface, vii.

75. [E] foi isso que João Guimarães Rosa me ensinou, é que um escritor tem a liberdade de criar uma linguagem que não seja a que os seus personagens utilizam: um homólogo desses personagens, dessa linguagem. Quero dizer, o que eu tinha que aprender do povo eram os mesmos processos com que ele constrói a sua linguagem . . . utilizando os mesmos processos conscientes ou inconscientes de que o povo serve para utilizar a língua portuguesa. From Laban, "Encontros," 27–29.

76. See Michel Laban, "L'Oeuvre Litterarie de Luandino Vieira." Laban's dissertation includes an extensive glossary based in part on a questionnaire he sent Luandino

Vieira concerning the origins of several hundred words in the author's narratives. Laban estimates that 70 percent of Luandino's neologisms are derived from Portuguese, while only 25 percent are from Kimbundu. While the glossary distinguishes popular luandense Portuguese from standard usage, Laban's calculations are not indicative of this distinction. Furthermore, he does not account for those neologisms formed through creolization and cites "mexebundo," for example, as of only Portuguese origin.

77. Luandino Vieira, *Luuanda*, 25, 29, 31.

78. Ornelas, "Luandino Vieira," 73.

79. Mestre-de-obras, sô Gil Afonso! Aiuê, mestre, rikolombolo riokulu, se riolobanga, jipisa jondoba suka-é! Luandino Vieira, *Velhas Estórias*, 16.

80. Elá, muadié. Proibido no decreto! Quimbundo não é oficial! . . . Ngueta kazuelê kimbundu sukuama! Luandino Vieira, *Velhas Estórias*, 17.

81. How's it going, boss? . . . I am a polyglot, I speak languages, boss. This here is French. Polyglot! In the trash, is where I'll put you next time. Luandino Vieira, *Velhas Estórias*, 17. My translation here is literal, of course, and does not account for the wonderful plays on words and languages in the original.

82. Sobral viu bem muadié estava ganhar, aquelas palavras todas eles não sabiam, marcavam pontos. Luandino Vieira, *Velhas Estórias*, 36.

83. Kaputu-é! Kaputu-é! Kaputu-é ka maka Se ka-tu-diê kavanza Uondoku-ru-dia ku maka. Luandino Vieira, *Velhas Estórias*, 41.

84. Salvato Trigo, in *Luandino Vieira*, 587, claims that Luandino Vieira transfers the atmosphere of the musseque—"o verdadeiro mosáico social e humano" (the true social and human mosaic)—to his text.

85. Foi aí que a mana Marília fitucou—como ia dizer a fiel Ximinha, quitandeira confidente de estado de alma em porta de quintal. Fitucou, é mesmo, não tem palavra alheia para sentir de musseque: raiva quente e palavrosa, de alma revirada para fora, as todas verdades ditas sem mais nem quê—mais amizade na zanga, menos ódio que cólera, como é, no vernáculo? Dona Marília, portanto, fitucou. Luandino Vieira, *Macandumba*, 84.

86. Alfredo Margarido, "Luandino," 63.

87. Zenith, *Loves*, 24. From Luandino Vieira, *João Vêncio*, 64: Banza-o léxico, o patuá! . . . Mas o meu pai é que me pôs o vício: ele me deu o dicionário aberto e fechado, estudei de cor. E depois meu musseque, as mil cores de gentes, mil vozes—eu gramo do putos 'verdianos, palavrinhas tchêu! E os rios da minha vida, minhas vias; que com marujos eu ainda fui cicerone de portas, pratos, pegas e prostitutas. "Gee! the clean dirty smell of this old she-rat . . . How much? Cem angolares? Vêncio, tell this old-crab I would rather f . . . myself . . . " Aiué, minhas munhungagens, sotaques.

88. Russell Hamilton, in "Black from White and White on Black," 52, explains that the use of "almost" in this way "strengthens the tension of reverse acculturation always repressed by the force of cultural racism."

89. Vou ter com Paizinho, vou encontrar com ele, contra todas as regras de segurança, contra a ordem que me deu. . . . E estou a trair, e é trair-lhe. Luandino Vieira, *Makulusu*, 121.

90. Temos de fazer o que fazemos mesmo que Maninho está-se a rir—e já não está, só está morto—e nos xingue que são jogos da sociedade, não tem mais outro caminho:

. . . lutar para que a tua razão nao seja razão e que tu vivas e Kibiaka viva e todos os mortos possam viver e os vivos morrer sem precisar de ser heróis. E de repente, me lembro agora na terceira palavra: kikunda, traição, é isso e digo:—Ukamba uakamba kikunda!— saímos no fundo da Morte do Makokaloji. E isso já não serve para nada: Paizinho está ali preso, ali a cento e poucos metros de mim. Luandino Vieira, *Makulusu*, 131.

91. Hoje, Tetembuatubia nem que é o simples nome na parede do tempo. . . . Mas aí foi a vida, inteira, o onde que a gente demos encontro os milagres do impossível, num antigamente longe. Luandino Vieira, *No Antigamente*, 14.

92. Na parede do tempo, Luanda que ia ser só um murmurido som de águas nas pedras duras lá da ilha dele, nos regressos. Luandino Vieira, *Macandumba*, 139.

93. Cidade de verdade que não existe mais, nunca mais, só em terra longe, um dia, que se pode dar encontro. E, aí, nem é nada que vimos, que vivemos—é a outra coisa, luz velada que no coração está morar, um orvalhado sereno cacimbo nos dentros de quem está exilado. Luandino Vieira, *Macandumba*, 139.

Chapter 3. Mimicry in the Contact Zone

1. Homi Bhabha, *Locations of Culture*, 87.

2. Américo G., "Uanhenga Xitu!," 3: A cidade está esgotada e há outras penas que podem falar da vida da cidade. Eu continuarei a falar do mato, das coisas do mato, porque muitos dos nossos camaradas desconhecem o que lá se passa e o que lá existe. . . . Vou continuar a falar de coisas como por exemplo do alambamento. Não como se faz hoje, que não é nada. . . . Temos de encarar de frente a nossa realidade cultural. A nossa literatura é oral, ela é fundamentalmente guardada pelos velhos e eles estão a morrer. Com eles morre também a grande riqueza cultural africana (angolana).

3. Mary Louise Pratt, *Imperial Eyes*, 7.

4. Mary Louise Pratt, "Criticism in the Contact Zone," 88.

5. Faço lembrar que o *"Mestre" Tamoda* foi apanhado duas vezes e queimado pelas autoridades da cadeia da Casa da Reclusão de Angola e do Tarrafal. Xitu, "Inquérito," 5.

6. O novo intelectual, no meio de uma sanzala em que quase todos os seus habitantes falavam quimbundo e só em casos especiais usavam o português, achou-se uma sumidade da língua de Camões. Uanhenga Xitu, *Tamoda*, 10.

7. Tinha sido denunciado como mandrião e sem documentos. Também o facto de alcunhar os cipaios de verdugos ou fintilhos, e aos quimbares (regedores) de panaças, de pacaios, criara-lhe antipatia junto das autoridades. Independemente disso, os frisos de cabelos que introduzira na gente nova, para ter o cabelo igual ao seu, provocavam queimaduras na cabeça. Uanhenga Xitu, *Tamoda*, 25.

8. Bhabha, *Locations of Culture*, 86.

9. See for example, Fernando Martinho, "Review of '*Mestre' Tamoda*," 478–79. Martinho claims that Tamoda defends the pride of a people who are capable of confusing the enemies in their own territory. Similarly, David Brookshaw argues that Tamoda democratizes the Portuguese language, in "Identidade e Ambivalência," 2–4.

10. Manuel Rui Monteiro, "Prefácio do Escritor Manuel Rui," 155.

11. Salvato Trigo, "Xitu," 32.

12. Ibid., 31.

13. Russell Hamilton, *Literatura Africana*, 221. David Brookshaw cites only three linguistic levels—Portuguese, Kimbundu, and Portuguese spoken by Africans, which he terms "neoportuguês" (2).

14. Uanhenga Xitu, personal interview, July 23, 1985.

15. É assim que hoje vemos pretos e mulatos civilizados a casarem-se com primas co-irmãs e com sobrinhas, ante a admiração das velhas que consideram isso kisunji (abominação, incesto), ou crime da morte para quem o praticasse na era dos seus antepassados. Uanhenga Xitu, *Discursos*, 51.

16. Estes gajos das Missões, quando se infiltram nas coisas da terra, provocam sempre distúrbios. Uanhenga Xitu, "Bola Com Feitiço," 69.

17. Uanhenga Xitu, "Bola Com Feitiço," 52.

18. Hamilton, *Literatura Africana*, 225.

19. Uanhenga Xitu, "Bola com Feitiço," 51.

20. Quando me lembro de estampar uma história ou conto no papel, o sentimento de que me rodeio é convencer-me de que estou diante de ouvintes que aguardam com entusiasmo o momento de me escutar e de me julgar. Uanhenga Xitu, *Maka*, 9.

21. Então, arranjo uma posição cómoda para melhor narrar a história, sem atender a que, no meio da minha gente, há alguns auditores que me podem influenciar, inibindo-me de continuar a narração. Uanhenga Xitu. *Maka*, 9.

22. E, em seguida, falo-lhes na linguagem mais chã, que é a minha: pobre de adjectivos, de vocabulário, de frases e palavras pomposas, e sem aquele rigor dos sinais de pontuação, porque tudo isso subsitutuo com gestos e partes só minhas. Uanhenga Xitu, *Maka*, 9.

23. Prezados leitores, vejo-me obrigado a apresentar-vos primeiramente a Mafuta e suas Mafutas, enquanto a velha Kasexi matabicha na casa do Toko. Porém, não se esqueçam de ligar o fio a esta interrupção quando chegar a devida altura. Uanhenga Xitu, *Maka*, 47.

24. Talvez os leitores estejam a lembrar-se da velha Kasexi, de Botomona, que, numa noite, foi até a Colomboloca para assistir um parto na casa do velho Toko. Uanhenga Xitu, *Maka*, 122.

25. Este sermão . . . foi feito num quimbundo tão puro e num tom filosófico que merecia uma tradução correspondente em português. Uanhenga Xitu, *Maka*, 126.

26. Manuel Rui, "Review of *Vozes na Sanzala*," 10.

27. Quer tivesses nascido do ventre de uma mulher, quer concebido pela minha imaginação e parido pela minha cabeça, presto-te homenagem, ao colocar no teu túmulo uma lápide, com esta inscrição. Uanhenga Xitu, *Vozes na Sanzala*, 233.

28. Mas *livrário* é quê?—Livrário é como uma pessoa que 'falou só mas não disse nada.' Uanhenga Xitu, *Manana*, 13.

29. Russell Hamilton also claims that Xitu's use of the term should be seen as a type of authorial self-deprecation and literary anticonventionalism. *Literatura Africana*, 232.

30. Às minhas amigas e amigos das camisarias, das oficinas de carpintaria, de alfaiataria, de serralharia, de sapataria, da fábrica de papel, lavadeiras, quitandeiras de quindas na cabeça, pedreiros—todos aqueles que andavam comigo e não falavam português do liceu. Uanhenga Xitu, *Manana*, 11.

31. Vocês vão ver: este livrário não tem português caro, não. Português do liceu, não. Do Dr., não. Do funcionário, não. De escritório, não. Só tem mesmo português d'agente mesmo, lá do bairro, lá da sanzala, lá do quimbo. Uanhenga Xitu, *Manana*, 15.

32. A vida deles é só ter sapato engraxado e camisa limpo. Mas em casa só comem farinha com açúcar. Mesmo o mano já viu quantos dotores pretos? Dotor preto só os santomês. Uanhenga Xitu, *Manana*, 28.

33. Os protestantes que cantavam o 'Sivayá. Sivayá . . . ,' e marchando num passo de procissão, dirigiam-se a uma classe. E atrás deles muitos e muitos assistentes. Aproveitando o som da música tão melodiosa e religiosa, alguns deles mungumanavam mbundas em cadência de batuque. Uanhenga Xitu, *Manana*, 119.

34. Fernando Martinho, Review of *Manana*, 96.

35. Ibid.

36. Felito Bata da Silva, Marceneiro, Africa. Ocid. Portuguesa, Angola. Uanhenga Xitu, *Manana*, 49.

37. Russell Hamilton notes that naming the baby Manana serves as a type of cultural resistance against imposed Portuguese customs, but at the same time the name sounds somewhat Christian. *Literatura Africana*, 223.

38. Vim à procura de uma garota chamada Manana, também conhecida por Ana, Mana Ana, Mariana, neta do velho Mbengu. Uanhenga Xitu, *Manana*, 124.

39. The term *máquina colonial* (colonial machine) was a commonly used metaphor to describe the Portuguese socioeconomic and political colonial apparatus.

40. Hamilton, *Literatura Africana*, 224.

41. [C]ontinuar a obra começada há séculos por heróis e bravos do passado para um Portugal maior. Uanhenga Xitu, *Os Sobreviventes*, 38.

42. Literatura fazem os homens possuídos de muita bagagem académica. . . . Ao passo que nós, que o nosso liceu foi no arranjo da estrada, carregar sacos, apanhar algodão, rachar lenhas, e o pagamento bofetada e pontapé no rabo, pela máquina colonial, e a Universidade foi a cadeia, compreende-se, portanto, que o mais podemos oferecer aos leitores são as imagens que recolhemos durante esses anos de observação directa de factos vividos na sanzala, sem preocuparmo-nos com rendilhados e o estilo de bom português de verdadeiros escritores. Sou escritor de MULALA NA MBUNDA, misturando português, quimbundo e umbundo. Procuramos escrever de forma possível a ser compreendidos pelos leitores que se identificam com a nossa linguagem e forma de viver. Uanhenga Xitu, *Os Sobreviventes*, 13.

43. Hamilton, *Literatura Africana*, 224.

44. Trigo, "Xitu," 30.

45. Há dias ouvi-te falar que o rapaz tinha sanque azul! . . . Deve ter mas é sangue dos Mouros ou dos negros, dos milhares de escravos que serviram os reis antigos. Uanhenga Xitu, *Os Sobreviventes*, 36.

46. Castro Soromenho (1910–1968) was born in Mozambique of Portuguese parents and raised in Angola. His trilogy denounces Portuguese colonialism as a dehumanizing project.

47. In my interview with Uanhenga Xitu, he verified that he had not read Castro Soromenho's novels prior to writing *Os Sobreviventes da Máquina Colonial Depõem*.

. . . In *Os Discursos do "Mestre" Tamoda*, however, there is reference to "Chagas" by Castro Soromenho (76).

Chapter 4. Visions of Utopia, Counternarrations of Nation

1. Homi Bhabha, *Locations of Culture*, 147.

2. *As Aventuras de Ngunga* was first published in 1973 by the Serviço de Cultura do MPLA (cultural sector of the MPLA) in the Frente Leste (Eastern Front).

3. The term *pioneiro* first referred to an MPLA youth organization. Later, it came to signify children in general.

4. Maria Teresa Gil Mendes da Silva, "As Aventuras de Ngunga," 594–609.

5. Fernando da Costa Andrade, *Literatura Angolana*.

6. Não serás, afinal, tu? Não será numa parte desconhecida de ti próprio que se esconde modestamente o pequeno Ngunga? Pepetela, *As Aventuras de Ngunga*, 128

7. Fernando Martinho, "Muana Puó," 434.

8. Ibid., 437.

9. Os morcegos compreenderam então que Deus era uma invenção dos corvos, com o que os tinham desde sempre subjugado pra terem o mel sem trabalhar. Pepetela, *Muana Puó*, 48

10. Henrique Abranches, *Reflexões sobre Cultura Nacional*, 22.

11. See also Manuel dos Santos Lima, *As Lágrimas e o Vento*. Santos Lima's novel focuses on an Angolan officer in the Portuguese army who joins the ranks of the clandestine nationalist movement in Luanda.

12. V.N., "Colóquio sobre *Mayombe*" (Colloquium on *Mayombe*), 3.

13. O problema no fundo é nacional—que nação é essa? Pepetela, interview with the author, July 15, 1985.

14. Aos guerrilheiros do Mayombe/que ousaram desafiar os deuses/abrindo um caminho na floresta obscura/Vou contar a história de Ogun/o Prometeu africano. Pepetela, *Mayombe*, 11.

15. Harold Courlander, *Tales of Yoruba Gods and Heroes*, 33–37.

16. Wole Soyinka, *Myth, Literature and the African World*, 30.

17. Obviously the militants' names have both experiential and allegorical significance. Enio Morães Dutra lists the noms de guerre of the different characters and explains their significance in "A Literatura Angolana," 167–78.

18. Nasci na Gabela, na terra do café. . . . Trago em mim o inconciliável e é este o meu motor. Num Universo de sim ou não, branco ou negro, eu represento o talvez. Pepetela, *Mayombe*, 16.

19. Estou no Mayombe . . . com o fim de arranjar no Universo maniqueísta o lugar para o talvez. Pepetela, *Mayombe*, 22.

20. E nós, os da Primeira Região, forçados a fazer a guerra aqui, numa região alheia, onde não falam a nossa língua, onde o povo é contra-revolucionário, e nós que fazemos aqui? Pepetela, *Mayombe*, 41.

21. Onde eu nasci, havia homens de todas as línguas vivendo nas casas comuns e miseráveis da Companhia. Onde eu cresci, no Bairro Benfica, em Benguela, havia homens de todas as línguas, sofrendo as mesmas amarguras. O primeiro bando a que

pertenci tinha mesmo meninos brancos, e tinha miúdos nascidos de pai umbundo, tchokue, kimbundo, fiote, kuanhama. . . . Querem hoje que eu seja tribalista! De que tribo, se eu sou de todas as tribos, não só de Angola, como de África? Pepetela, *Mayombe*, 139.

22. Eu sou o tipo que nunca poderia pertencer ao aparelho. Eu sou o tipo cujo papel histórico termina quando ganharmos a guerra. Pepetela, *Mayombe*, 261.

23. Sem Medo resolveu o seu problema fundamental: para se manter ele próprio, teria de ficar ali, no Mayombe. Terá nascido demasiado cedo ou demasiado tarde? Em todo o caso fora do seu tempo, como qualquer herói de tragédia. Pepetela, *Mayombe*, 285.

24. V.N., "Colóquio sobre *Mayombe*," 4.

25. [S]e na altura o livro não podia ser utilizado pelos inimigos do MPLA quando a independência ainda não foi consolidada. Pepetela, interview with the author.

26. Porque com uma introdução, uma parte da mensagem do livro será perdida. Essa de fazer as pessoas pensar pela sua própria cabeça. From V.N., "Colóquio sobre *Mayombe*," 5.

27. *Yaka* was to have been published simultaneously in Brazil by Editora Ática and in Portugal by Dom Quixote. The Portuguese edition was delayed.

28. Yaka, Mbayaka, jaga, imbangala? Foram uma mesma formação social(?), Nação(?)—aos antropólogos de esclarecer. . . . Criadores de chefias, assimiladores de culturas, formadores de exércitos com jovens de outras populações que iam integrando na sua caminhada, parecem uma idéia, errante, cazumbi, antecipado da nacionalidade. Pepetela, *Yaka*, 6.

29. Margret Ammann and José Carlos Venâncio, "Pepetela," 6–7. In this interview, Pepetela comments on both the nationalist and anticolonial role of Jaga statuary.

30. Está onde? Os miúdos até desaprenderam o nome dele. Não há nome que fica quando o comboio inglês avança. Pepetela, *Yaka*, 72.

31. *Brancos da segunda classe* (second-class whites) was the pejorative term commonly used to describe Angolan-born whites, in contrast to *brancos da primeira classe* (first-class whites).

32. Sempre fomos homens cegos e fracos a querer travar as tempestades com as mãos. Acreditando ser heróis. Heróis do mar, Nação valente e imortal. . . . Não é isso que diz o Hino? . . . E espalhamos a fé cristã. . . . Só sabemos recitar lições decoradas. E o grave é que acreditamos nelas. Pepetela, *Yaka*, 202.

33. Bem, já posso fechar estes olhos transparentes que tantas coisas viram. Minha criação está aí em torrentes de esperança, a anunciada chegou. Posso então me desequilibrar do soco e ficar em cacos pelo chão, a boca para um lado, os olhos pelo mar, o coração embaixo da terra, o sexo para o Norte e as pernas para o Sul? Ou será melhor aguardar ainda? Pepetela, *Yaka*, 302.

34. *O Cão e os Caluandas* (1985) will be discussed briefly in chapter 5 on Manuel Rui's works in a comparative context. This text, like Manuel Rui's postcolonial narratives, focuses on the realities and languages of nation-building in Luanda.

35. David Mestre, "Um Livro Exemplar," 7. Mestre suggests that Dinoluan is an anagram of Luandino. His column on *Lueji* was written before the book was published and speaks of the forthcoming novel by Pepetela.

36. É certo que há versões contraditórias. Como tudo na tradição oral. Cada grupo deforma uma versão em função dos seus interesses." Pepetela, *Lueji*, 376.

37. With independence, the tendency has been to substitute the Portuguese "qu" with "k." Hence the new spellings of *kitandeira* (quitandeira) and *kimbanda* (quimbanda).

38. UPA is the acronym for the União dos Povos Angolanos (Union of Angolan Peoples), one of the original nationalist liberation groups that later became the FNLA (Frente Nacional para a Libertação de Angola) under the leadership of Holden Roberto.

39. Somos nós, com a guerra em Angola, que vamos derrubar o fascismo. Esta é a maka. Pepetela, *Utopia*, 52.

40. E lá vinham as cristianíssimas cruzes de Cristo, pintadas a vermelha, nas barrigas dos bombeiros, tingir de vermelho rasgado as barrigas negras das crianças. Pepetela, *Utopia*, 124.

41. Vivo nestas matas há cinco anos, falo a língua daqui, amei com todo o respeito uma mulher do Leste, cuja morte me matou. Sou mesmo do Norte? Nunca me vi assim, sou apenas angolano. Pepetela, *Utopia*, 143.

42. Pensávamos que íamos construir uma sociedade justa, sem diferenças, sem privilégios. . . . E depois tudo se adulterou, tudo apodreceu, muito antes de se chegar ao poder. . . . A utopia morreu. E hoje cheira mal, como qualquer corpo em putrefacção. Pepetela, *Utopia*, 202.

43. Esse colono vai pagar. Esses muadiés vêm lá de fora e pensam que mandam em nós, que nos podem roubar e bater. Tempo do colono acabou. Pepetela, *Utopia*, 294.

44. Como é obvio, não pode existir epílogo nem ponto final para uma estória que começa por portanto. Pepetela, *Utopia*, 316.

Chapter 5. After the Revolution

1. The distinction made by the first and second liberation struggles (*primeira e segunda guerras de libertação*) is one made by the MPLA. The first liberation war refers to the nationalist struggle against the Portuguese. Combat after 1974 among FNLA, MPLA, and UNITA forces and each movement's respective supporters is known as the second liberation struggle.

2. Integrava uma classe de pretos bem vestidos, falando bom português, recebendo por isso o apodo de calcinhas. Manuel Rui, *Regresso Adiado*, 72.

3. De sobressair o sangue do seu pai da indelével mistura com o sangue que a mãe herdara de gente escrava. Manuel Rui, *Regresso Adiado*, 43.

4. Fulano a pensar que Vintesete e Mateus antes não tinham nome, incorre em gravíssimo erro histórico de quem não sabe que tinham sim, mas que eram nomes boçais, nomes de pretos, sem música, sem número, sem Ribeiro ou versículo bíblico Mateus trinta e tal. Manuel Rui, *Regresso Adiado*, 105.

5. Russell Hamilton, for instance, finds that Manuel Rui's codification of a language linked intimately to the period and new sociopolitical order is at the center of his fiction. Hamilton, *Literatura Africana*, 92.

6. *Sim Camarada!* has been translated into English as *Yes, Comrade!* by Ronald Sousa. All translations of quotes come from this text and will be cited in the notes by page number.

7. Sousa, *Yes, Comrade!* 8. From Manuel Rui, *Sim Camarada!* 16: O leitor que não sabe fica a saber que este governo era internacional. Tinha partes. A angolana, a portuguesa, a americana, a francesa, a zairota, alemã e a etecétera.

8. Sousa, *Yes, Comrade!* 10. From Manuel Rui, *Sim Camarada!* 18: Outra vez com as aumentações do 'poder popular'? É melhor interrompermos a sessão para o café.

9. Sousa, *Yes, Comrade!* 53. From Manuel Rui, *Sim Camarada!* 73: Eu não vou na cama com gente que fala francês!

10. The original text states that Mana Domingas is *caminhando livre.* The English translation of "walking along" is literally correct but loses that sense of freedom gained with the assumption of collective identity.

11. Russell Hamilton notes that the "sim camarada" motif functions as a means of supplanting other titles, which divide along class lines. Hamilton, *Literatura Africana,* 193.

12. Sousa, *Yes, Comrade!* 90. From Manuel Rui, *Sim Camarada!* 122: A linguagem estava codificada. Imperialismo, neocolonialismo, fantoches, lacaios, poder popular, eram palavras de andar de boca em boca.

13. Sousa, *Yes, Comrade!* 3. Manuel Rui, *Sim Camarada!* 11: a página da história está virada. Era só pôr cuspo no dedo, agarrar aí a página e pronto!

14. Manuel Rui's first collection of poems, published in 1973, is entitled *A Onda* (The wave). In his introduction to the English translation of *Sim Camarada!*, Gitahi Gititi discusses the writer's use of the sea as a trope for the possible futures of Angola. Gitahi Gititi, foreword, *Yes, Comrade!*, ix–xxvi.

15. O mar é uma coisa sempre igual e sempre a mudar. Manuel Rui, interview with the author, July 18, 1985.

16. Nada permanence que não seja/para a necessária mudança./Que o diga o mar. Manuel Rui, *Cinco Vezes Onze,* 111.

17. The sea here becomes an ambivalent figure, as a trope for the imaginings of nation and for colonial history. Agostinho Neto, in *Náusea,* also evokes the ambivalence of the sea as the life force of Angola and as the water path of colonization and enslavement.

18. [O] que foi a grande traição de vinte cinco de Abril. Manuel Rui, *Memória do Mar,* 80. The Portuguese New State was overthrown on April 25, 1974.

19. Senhores, ordena-me el-rei por graça, que imponhamos a fé ao infiel e a civilização ao gentio que em troca nos deverá pagar o insignificante e material tributo de canela, do ouro e do marfim. Manuel Rui, *Memória do Mar,* 99.

20. The literal translation is "order words," but palavras de ordem specify the phrases used by MPLA militants as part of the revolutionary world view. In this sense, they also were a type of revolutionary public discourse.

21. Descuple camarada Nazário, mas suino é com ésse, disciplina é antes de vigilância e antes da luta continua tem de pôr pelo Poder Popular e no fim acaba ano da criação da Assembleia do Povo e Congresso Extraordinário do Partido! Manuel Rui, *Quem Me Dera,* 29.

22. Ao nosso carnaval/havemos de voltar. Agostinho Neto, "Havemos de Voltar," 130.

23. The term *caluandas* is used to distinguish inhabitants of the city of Luanda from *gente da ilha,* those who live in Luanda's island section.

24. O sacana era masé um lumpen, anbancou o meu almoço, dorumiu, quando acordou foi à vida. Sem despedir. Um parasita, um explorador. E eu, Tico, um intelectual revolucionário, não fiz o tal poema que pensei. O sacrista não merecia, continuava com a mentalidade de burguês, inimigo de classe dum operarió-camponês como eu, cinco séculos explorado. Pepetela, *O Cão e os Caluandas,* 16.

25. The closest literal translation of mujimbo is "rumor." This does not capture the derivation of the Angolan word, which, as one of the characters in *Crónica de um Mujimbo* explains, is Tchokwe for "message." During the nationalist liberation struggle, "mujimbo" was appropriated by the guerrillas to signify any type of news, messages, intrigues, and so on, and came to mean an unconfirmed report or rumor. Manuel Rui, *Mujimbo,* 92.

26. The fado is a nostalgic, plaintive song style that emerged in Portugal at the end of the nineteenth century.

27. Transferência de tecnologia. Know how. Nova ordem económica internacional. Manuel Rui, *Mujimbo,* 86.

Bibliography

Abranches, Henrique. *Reflexões sobre Cultura Nacional* (Reflections on national culture). Lisbon: Edições 70, 1980.

Ammann, Margaret, and José Carlos Venâncio. "Pepetela, Um Construtor de Angolanidade" (Pepetela, a constructor of Angolanness). *Jornal de Letras, Artes e Ideias* 10, no. 430 (October 2–8, 1988): 6–7.

Anderson, Benedict. *Imagined Communities*. Rev. ed. London: Verso, 1991.

Anderson, Perry. "Portugal and the End of Ultra-Colonialism." *New Left Review* 15 (1962): 83–102; 16 (1962): 88–123; 17 (1962): 85–114.

Andrade, Fernando da Costa. *Literatura Angolana* (Angolan literature). Lisbon: Edições 70, 1980.

Andrade, Mário Pinto de. "Uma Nova Linguagem no Imaginário Angolano" (A new language in the Angolan imaginary). In Laban et al., *Luandino*, 219–27.

António, Mário. *Luanda, "Ilha" Crioula* (Luanda creole "island"). Lisbon: Agência Geral do Ultramar, 1968.

Assis Júnior, António. *O Segredo da Morta* (The secret of the dead woman). Lisbon: Edições 70, 1979.

Bender, Gerald. *Angola under the Portuguese: The Myth and the Reality*. Berkeley: University of California Press, 1978.

Bender, Tamara. Translator's preface to *Luuanda*, by José Luandino Vieira, v–x. London: Heinemann, 1980.

Bhabha, Homi. *Locations of Culture*. London: Routledge, 1994.

Boavida, Américo. *Angola: Cinco Séculos de Exploração Portuguesa* (Angola: five centuries of Portuguese exploitation). Lisbon: Edições 70, 1981.

Brookshaw, David. "Indentidade e Ambivalência em Uanhenga Xitu" (Identity and ambivalence in Uanhenga Xitu). *Angolê* (1988): 2–4.

Burness, Donald. *Fire: Six Writers from Angola, Mozambique and Cape Verde*. Washington: Three Continents Press, 1977.

Cabral, Amílcar. *National Liberation and Culture*. Syracuse: Syracuse University Press, 1970.

———. *Unidade e Luta* (Unity and struggle), vol. I, *A Arma da Teoria* (The weapon of theory). Lisbon: Seara Nova, 1976.

Chatelain, Héli, ed. *Folk Tales of Angola*. Boston: Houghton, Mifflin, 1894.

Courlander, Harold. *Tales of Yoruba Gods and Heroes.* New York: Crown Publishers, 1973.

Davidson, Basil. *In the Eye of the Storm: Angola's People.* Garden City, N.Y.: Doubleday, 1972.

Duffy, James. *Portugal in Africa.* Cambridge: Harvard University Press, 1962.

Dutra, Enio Morães. "A Literatura Angolana de Ênfase Social: O Exemplo de *Mayombe*" (Angolan literature of social emphasis: the example of *Mayombe*). *Letras de Hoje* 26, no. 1 (March 1991): 167–78.

Ervedosa, Carlos. "Cartas do Tarrafal" (Letters from Tarrafal). In Laban et al., *Luandino*, 83–103.

Fanon, Frantz. *The Wretched of the Earth.* New York: Grove Press, 1963.

Ferreira, Eduardo de Sousa. *O Fim de uma Era: O Colonialismo Português em Africa* (The end of an era: Portuguese colonialism in Africa). Lisbon: Livraria Sá da Costa, Editora, 1977.

Ferreira, Manuel, ed. *No Reino de Caliban-II* (In the realm of Caliban-II). Lisbon: Seara Nova, 1976.

Ferreira, Manuel. Preface to *A Cidade e a Infância* (The city and childhood), by José Luandino Vieira, 2d ed., Lisbon: Edições 70, 1978.

Freyre, Gilberto. *Portuguese Integration in the Tropics.* Lisbon: Tipografia Silva, 1961.

G., Américo. "Uanhenga Xitu! Vem do Brasil Sorpreendido com a Popularidade de *Mestre Tamoda*" ("Uanhenga Xitu! returns from Brazil surprised by the popularity of *Mestre Tamoda*). *Vida e Cultura* 30 (October 1983): 4–5.

Gititi, Gitahi. Foreword to *Yes, Comrade!* Ronald Sousa, trans. Minneapolis: University of Minnesota Press, 1993.

Hall, Stuart. "Cultural Identity and Diaspora." In Jonathan Rutherford, ed., *Identity, Community, Culture, Difference.* London: Lawrence & Wishart, 1990.

Hamilton, Russell. "Black from White and White on Black: Contradictions of Language in the Angolan Novel." *Ideologies and Literatures.* (December 1976–January 1977): 25–58.

———. *Literatura Africana, Literatura Necessária I—Angola* (African literature, necessary literature I—Angola). Lisbon: Edições 70, 1981.

———. *Voices from an Empire.* Minneapolis: University of Minnesota Press, 1975.

Harlow, Barbara. *Resistance Literature.* New York: Metheun, 1987.

Laban, Michel. "Encontro com a Literatura Angolana." *Vértice* (September–October 1984): 67–80.

———. "Encontros com Luandino Vieira" (Meetings with Luandino Vieira). In Laban et al., *Luandino*, 9–82.

———. "L'Oeuvre Litteraire de Luandino Vieira" (Literary work of Luandino Vieira). Ph.D. diss., L'Univérsité de Paris–Sorbonne, 1979.

———. "Quadro Cronológico de Obra de Luandino Vieira" (Chronological chart of the work of Luandino Vieira). In Laban et al., *Luandino*, 312.

Laban, Michel, et al. *Luandino: José Luandino Vieira e sua obra* (Luandino: José Luandino Vieira and his work). Lisbon: Edições 70, 1980.

Laranjeira, Pires. "Luandino Vieira—Apresentação da Vida Verdadeira" (Luandino Vieira—presentation of the real life). *Vozes* (March 1979): 85–96.

Lepecki, Maria Lúcia. "Luandino Vieira: Sob o Signo da Verdade" (Luandino Vieira: under the sign of truth). *Africa* 2 (1978): 134–42.

Lima, Manuel dos Santos. *As Lógrimas e o Vento* (The tears and the wind). Lisbon: Africa Editora, 1975.

Margarido, Alfredo. "Luandino: Retrato de Ambaquista João Vêncio" (Luandino: portrait of the ambaquista João Vêncio). *Colóquio/Letras* 61 (1981): 63–67.

Marquês, Carlos Vaz. "Luandino: 'Português é um Trofeu de Guerra'" (Luandino: "Portuguese is a war trophy"). *Jornal de Letras, Artes e Ideias* 9, no. 357 (May 9–15, 1989): 8–9.

Martinho, Fernando. "Muana Puó—Enigma e Metamorfose" (Muana Puó—enigma and metamorphosis). *Africa* 4 (1979): 434–38.

———. Preface to *João Vêncio: Os Seus Amores*, by José Luandino Vieira. Lisbon: Edições 70, 1979.

———. Review of *Manana*, by Uanhenga Xitu. *Africa* 1 (1978): 96.

———. Review of *"Mestre" Tamoda e Outros Contos*, by Uanhenga Xitu. *Africa* 4 (1979): 478–79.

Mensagem. Ed. Departmento da Associação dos Naturais de Angola, Luanda, 1951–52, nos. 1–4.

Mestre, David. "Um Livro Exemplar" (An exemplary book). *Jornal de Letras, Artes e Ideias* 8, no. 326 (October 4–10, 1988): 7.

Monteiro, Manuel Rui. "Prefácio do Escritor Manuel Rui Monteiro para uma Reedição do Livro 'Mestre' Tamoda e Outros Contos" (Preface by the writer Manuel Rui Monteiro for a re-edition of the book "Mestre" Tamoda and other stories). In Uanhenga Xitu, *Os Sobreviventes da Máquina Colonial Depõem . . .* , 155–57.

Moser, Gerald M. *Essays in Portuguese-African Literature*. University Park: Pennsylvania State University Press, 1969.

N., V. "Colóquio Sobre 'Mayombe': Um Livro Para Despertar o Leitor" (Colloquium on "Mayombe": a book to awaken the reader). *Lavra & Oficina* (October–December 1980): 3–5.

Neto, Agostinho. *Ainda o Meu Sonho* (Yet my dream). Luanda: União dos Escritores Angolanos, 1980.

———. "Havemos de Voltar" (We must return). In *Sagrada Esperança* (Sacred hope), by Agostinho Neto. 9th ed. Lisbon: Livraria Sá da Costa, 1979, 130.

———. *Naúsea*. Lisbon: Edições 70, 1980.

Ornelas, José. "José Luandino Vieira: A Desconstrução do Discurso Colonial" (José Luandino Vieira: the deconstruction of colonial discourse). *Letras de Hoje* (June 1990): 59–82.

Pepetela. *As Aventuras de Ngunga* (The adventures of Ngunga). Lisbon: Publicações Dom Quixote, 1976.

———. *A Geração da Utopia* (The generation of utopia). Lisbon: Publicações Dom Quixote, 1992.

———. Interview with the author. Luanda, July 12, 1985.

———. *Lueji*. Luanda: União dos Escritores Angolanos, 1989.

———. *Mayombe*. Lisbon: Edições 70, 1982.

———. *Muana Puó*. Lisbon: Edições 70, 1978.

———. *O Cão e os Caluandas* (The dog and the Caluandas). Lisbon: Publicações Dom Quixote, 1985.

———. *O Desejo de Kianda* (The desire of Kianda). Lisbon: Publicações Dom Quixote, 1995.

———. *Yaka*. São Paulo: Editora Ática, 1984.

Pratt, Mary Louise. "Criticism in the Contact Zone: De-centering Community and Nation." In Stephen Bell, Albert LeMay, and Leonard Orr, eds., *Culture, Politics, and Latin American Narrative*. South Bend, Ind.: University of Notre Dame Press, 1993.

———. *Imperial Eyes*. London: Routledge, 1992.

Rosa, João Guimarães. *Grande Sertão: Veredas* (Great hinterland: paths). 11th ed. Rio de Janeiro: José Olympio Editora S.A., 1976.

———. *Sagarana*. 20th ed. Rio de Janeiro: José Olympio Editora S.A., 1977.

Rui, Manuel. *Cinco Vezes Onze* (Five times eleven). Lisbon: Edições 70, 1985.

———. *Crónica De Um Mujimbo* (Chronicle of a rumor). Luanda: União dos Escritores Angolanos, 1989.

———. Interview with the author, taped, Luanda, July 18, 1985.

———. *Memória do Mar* (Memory of the sea). Luanda: União dos Escritores Angolanos, 1980.

———. *1 Morto e Os Vivos* (One corpse and the living). Lisbon: Edições Cotovia, 1993.

———. *Quem Me Dera Ser Onda* (If only I were a wave). Lisbon: Edições 70, 1982.

———. *Regresso Adiado* (Delayed return). Luanda. União dos Escritores Angolanos, 1978.

———. Review of *Vozes na Sanzala*, by Uanhenga Xitu. *Lavra & Oficina* 1–3, reprint (1981): 9–10.

———. *Sim Camarada!* Lisbon: Edições 70, 1977.

———. *Yes, Comrade!*. Ronald Sousa, trans. Minneapolis: University of Minnesota Press, 1993.

Said, Edward. *Culture and Imperialism*. New York: Knopf, 1993.

Shohat, Ella. "Notes on the Post-Colonial." *Social Text* 31/32 (1992): 99–114.

Silva, Maria Teresa Gil Mendes da. "As Aventuras de Ngunga—Uma Mitologia Invertida" (The Adventures of Ngunga—An Inverted Mythology?). *Africa* (Rome) vol. 10, 1980.

Sommer, Doris. "Resisting the Heat." In Amy Kaplan and Donald Pense, eds., *Cultures of United States Imperialism*. Durham, N.C.: Duke University Press, 1993.

Soyinka, Wole. *Myth, Literature and the African World*. Cambridge: Cambridge University Press, 1976.

Spivak, Gayatri. "Can the Subaltern Speak?" In Larry Grossberg and Cary Nelson, eds., *Marxism and the Interpretation of Cultures*. Urbana: University of Illinois Press, 1987, 271–313.

Trigo, Salvato. *Luandino Vieira o Logoteta* (Luandino Vieira the inventor of words). Porto, Portugal: Brasília Editora, 1981.

———. Preface to *Os Discursos do "Mestre" Tamoda* (The discourses of "Master" Tamoda), by Uanhenga Xitu. Luanda: União dos Escritores Angolano e Instituto Nacional do Livro e do Disco, 1985, 13–18.

———. "Uanhenga Xitu—da Oratura à Literatura" (Uanhenga Xitu—from orature to literature). *Cadernos de Literatura* 12 (1982): 29–33.

Vieira, José Luandino. "Acho Que Já Trabalhei Um Bocado" (I think I've already worked a bit). *Lavra & Oficina* (April–May 1980): 8–11.

———. "Canção para Luanda." In Manuel Ferreira, ed., *No Reino de Caliban - II*, 239–41.

———. *A Cidade e a Infância* (The city and childhood). 2d ed. Lisbon: Edições 70, 1978.

———. Interviews with the author, taped, Luanda, July 16, 21, and 25, 1985.

———. *João Vêncio: Os Seus Amores*. Lisbon: Edições 70, 1979.

———. *The Loves of João Vêncio*. Richard Zenith, trans. New York: Harcourt Brace Jovanovitch, 1991.

———. *Lourentinho Dona Antónia de Sousa Neto e Eu*. Lisbon: Edições 70, 1981.

———. *Luuanda*. 8th ed. Lisbon: Edições 70, 1981.

———. *Luuanda*. Tamara Bender, trans. London: Heinemann, 1980.

———. *Macandumba*. Lisbon: Edições 70, 1978.

———. *No Antigamente, Na Vida* (In the long ago, in life). Lisbon: Edições 70, 1977.

———. *Nós, os do Makulusu* (We, those of Makulusu). Lisbon: Livraria Sá da Costa, 1977.

———. *Velhas Estórias* (Old estórias). Lisbon: Edições 70, 1976.

———. *A Vida Verdadeira de Domingos Xavier* (The real life of Domingos Xavier). Lisbon: Edições 70, 1977.

———. *Vidas Novas* (New lives). Lisbon: Edições 70, 1976.

Wheeler, Douglas, and René Pélissier. *Angola*. New York: Praeger, 1971.

Xitu, Uanhenga. "Inquérito aos Escritores." *Lavra & Oficina* (April 1982): 5.

———. Interview with the author, taped, Luanda, July 23, 1985.

———. *Manana*. Lisbon: Edições 70, 1979.

———. "*Mestre*" *Tamoda e Outros Contos* ("Master" Tamoda and other stories). Lisbon: Edições 70, 1977.

———. *O Ministro* (The minister). Luanda: União dos Escritores Angolanos, 1990.

———. *Os Discursos do "Mestre" Tamoda* (The discourses of "Master" Tamoda). Luanda: União dos Escritores Angolanos e Instituto Nacional do Livro e do Disco, 1984.

———. *Os Sobreviventes da Máquina Colonial Depõem . . .* (The survivors of the colonial machine testify . . .). Lisbon: Edições 70, 1980.

Index

PHILLIS PERES is associate professor of Spanish and Portuguese at the University of Maryland, College Park, and a regular contributor to various scholarly journals on African, Brazilian, and Portuguese literatures and colonial discourse.